1.00

The Soul of the Symbols

The Soul of the Symbols

A Theological Study of Holy Communion

by

JOSEPH R. SHULTZ

WILLIAM B. EERDMANS PUBLISHING COMPANY
GRAND RAPIDS, MICHIGAN

Printed in the United States of America
Library of Congress Catalog Card Number: 66-18723.

TO MY FAMILY

Preface

Holy Communion is an intense spiritual moment in a living faith, an unmistakable "touching" and "partaking" of the very God in Christ, a sense of sharing in the highest and purest worship of God. Many lives over the centuries attest to the fact of the reality of Holy Communion. The power and mystery of Holy Communion meant so much to the early Church, changing its life, and changing the world. We need to be painfully honest and rediscover, or discover for the first time, the "soul" of Holy Communion. Such is the purpose of this book.

Our Savior intended Holy Communion to be a very practical service from which His followers might derive powerful spiritual results. The splendor and glory and power of God are made available for us to realize and appropriate in an acted drama that all can enter into equally. We have never fully recognized nor realized the dynamic power available to us through Him who dwells within us. We are stunted spiritual pygmies, rather than spiritual giants living as sons of the almighty God. If the truth were told, we might be shaken to realize that Holy Communion has become a mere religious duty to many who merely fear death. To many, Holy Communion is neither refreshing nor strengthening; it is an outmoded service to be endured because it is the tradition of the Church. To many Christians, Holy Communion is neither "holy" nor "communion," but a secret disappointment. How absolutely tragic that this service of all Christian worship should revert to religious practice, to a mere sense of duty! Christ objected to religious rules and services which did not have practical spiritual meaning for the ordinary man. Jesus Christ was an absolutely practical person, desiring that man's spiritual quest should be realized and fulfilled, in Him. Thus the purpose of this study is to rediscover the "soul" of the sacramental symbols of the triune Holy Communion. This motive is not to form a new Christian doctrine, but to recharge a very old one.

Holy Communion is at the very center of Christian doctrine and Christian worship. However, some may question the relevancy of a new study in our day. In a world of missiles and rockets on the threshold of either the exploration of the heavens or the extermination of the earth, in a world of over-population and undernourishment, in a world that is witnessing the birth of new nations and the death of old nations, is the Holy Communion service of the Church that important? Is Holy Communion in the Christian faith vital in a nuclear age? The answer is that Christianity in the world today is impeded, not in power or in principle or in Person, but in practice. The Church does possess the answers for the world, but they are possessed within the Church rather than practiced in the world. A vital practice of the faith must include true belief in and observance of Holy Communion.

The Holy Communion is an epitome of the Gospel of Christ; it is the Gospel dramatized in a way that enables each believer inspired of God to live out his faith. Long before the early Church had New Testament Scriptures, buildings, or organization, it had the "breaking of bread." This breaking of bread was its worship service. The early Christians found in this very natural service supernatural strength. The early Church found in the practice of Holy Communion a powerful proclamation of the Gospel. The Church today can likewise realize power through the meaningful practice of Holy Communion.

This book is intended to be a bridge between theology and laity, to provide a vital link between the dogmatics of the faith and the practice of the faith. The book could have been limited to the one or the other, and written in a manner more general for the layman or more theological for the minister. It is quite apparent, however, that the already existing "theological curtain" between the laity (*laos*) and pastors (*poimenas*) is a mistake which hurts the work of the Kingdom of Christ. "Theology" is not intended to be a reserved area of study for the "profession." Laymen need to study more deeply and systematically the great truths of God in order to give a reason for the hope that abides in their hearts. Christian teachers in the programs of Christian education must understand the teachings of Christ and be able to communicate them to the students. God can use an ignorant man, but he cannot use his ignorance. The work of the Holy Spirit is potent in the Church today where laymen and minister together study the divine truth of God.

The historic reference of Christ and the early Church in Scripture determines the outline of the volume. Christ initiated the last night and all that transpired. Thus the burden of Chapter 1 must necessarily be the Person of God in Christ, the Host of Holy Communion. The invitation to Communion bears the name of Christ. The historic setting is considered next because the Last Supper took place during the Passover season. Christ's selection of the feast of Passover as the time of the inauguration of Holy Communion has sacred significance. After the Person of Christ and the setting have been established, His words and deeds are considered. Chapters 3, 4, and 5 deal with the distinct component parts of the triune Holy Communion. The order of Pedilavium, Love-Feast, and Eucharist follow the historic reference. These chapters seek to reveal the divine truth, "the soul," of the sacramental symbols of Holy Communion. In a sense they are the heart of the volume, as they are the heart of Communion. The study of the sacramental symbols of Communion leads one to a consideration of symbols in general. The invitation of Christ to Communion has an "R.S.V.P." The invited guest must be motivated to reply to the great invitation. The burden of the volume would not be fulfilled without this concluding chapter.

The relevancy of a study of Holy Communion in our day becomes apparent from the fact that the Church and the world are affected more by individual discipleship than by collective diplomacy. In this age of space it sounds naive to suggest that the tremendous world problems are but the accumulated reflection of individual problems and that the righteous morality and peace of collective society must have their source in the soul of individual man but it is true.

Another vital reason for a study of Holy Communion in our day is to enable our generation to affirm its faith and doctrine. The practice of the triune Holy Communion is questioned by some in our generation. They propose that the Christian faith and form of worship should be synchronized with the religions of the world, eliminating the Christian sacrament of Holy Communion. Within the membership of the Church there are some who are placing the supernatural on trial. This book attempts to demonstrate the unique revelation of God in Christ and the sacraments based upon this revelation.

The present volume is the result of a personal, independent investigation of this most exciting subject. I wrote the manuscript while studying at New College, University of Edinburgh, Scotland. It will undoubtedly reflect the thought of certain Christian teachers from this part of the Christian world. The New English Bible is used to a large extent where New Testament Scriptures are quoted.

Finally, believing that there is a need for a fresh study of the Holy Communion, I have dared to attempt to fill this need. Samuel Johnson once chided a preacher who planned a series of sermons for prisoners within the Tower of London, because a number of his hearers would be hanged before the services were completed. In the life of the Church, and of the world, there is not time to wait for the last word on a doctrine. The "eskaton" is present.

Contents

1

The Divine Appointment

The Host of Holy Communion

THE HOST OF HOLY COMMUNION IS CHRIST. HE IS THE ONE who has prepared this most sacred of worship services and it is He who invites us to enter into the community of God. The Gracious One has spread the board with the feast of salvation. God in Christ resides at the head of the communion table which is for all who accept His invitation of love by faith. This service in particular symbolizes the time when we enter into the family circle of God. Because it has been practiced for centuries there is often a deceptively common simplicity which shrouds the encounter with the living God. But it is always the way of God to meet us at the common place. Holy Communion is not a re-enactment of Calvary, but an unforgettable proclamation of the God whom we adore. Children of God, out of ordinary life, gather together in communion with the Father in the sacred mystery of this Holy Sacrament.

The Person of Jesus Christ is the essence of Holy Communion. Appreciation of the Lord's Supper is in direct relation to our appreciation of the Lord. The Lord of the Lord's Supper is the "a priori" who determines its practice. Holy Communion is not the simple furtherance of the "establishment," nor spiritual trickery, but genuine fellowship with the Risen One. Our chief concern is not doctrinal detail but divine fellowship with God in Christ.

The great invitation to communion with God comes from the Son. "Do this" rings across the centuries as the command of Jesus Christ. The community of believers, the Church, practices Holy Communion because of the Person, Jesus Christ. The Head and Host of every Holy Communion is God in Christ. He is the Divine One in the drama of Communion.

Because God was in Christ Holy Communion is a sacrament of His Church. Neither man nor angel has power to institute Holy Communion. No one has this power except God. Because God was in Christ we believe the words, "For this is my blood of the new testament, which is shed for many for the remission of sins" (Matt. 26:28). Because God was in Christ we take seriously the words, "Ye call me Master and Lord, and ye say well; for so I am. If I then, your Lord and Master, have washed your feet, ye also ought to wash one another's feet" (John 13:13, 14). If a man with power simply says go to his servant and he goes, how much more authoritative when God speaks and commands. God need not repeat His words to give them *weight* and *authority*. Either He is God and what He says is inescapable, divine command, or He is a demigod and all that He says is diabolical. However, we *know* that God was in Christ, and we know through the Person of Christ that God is love. We also know that the commands that come from a loving God are commands of love: "Happy are ye if ye do them" (John 13:17).

The position of man in the sacrament of Holy Communion is the position which the Apostle gives, "Christ's underlings and as stewards of the secrets of God" (I Cor. 4:1). We are mere stewards of that which God has done in Christ, ministers of holy things. No man or religious institution has the power to give or to retain Holy Communion. God has ordained this divine service.

The Person of Jesus Christ has taken upon Himself humanity; He has taken upon Himself our sin and death. Jesus Christ still bears this humanity, glorified, for He has never ceased to be human since He departed from this world. "For it is in Christ that the complete being of the Godhead dwells embodied (*somatikos*)" (Col. 2:9). He still bears the marks of the Cross, of our sins. In a sense He says to us as He said to Thomas, "Reach hither thy finger, and behold my hands; and reach hither thy hand and thrust it into my side, and be not faithless, but believing" (John 20:27). True Holy Communion brings one to adoration and confession of Him who loved us and gave Himself for us. It is communion of God with man, and man with God, through the Cross of Christ.

In the second century the Church father Clement wrote, "Brethren, we must think of Jesus Christ as of God. . . For He gave us light, He called us 'Son,' as a Father, He saved us when we were perishing."

The Person of Jesus Christ

The Person of Christ is the heart of the Christian faith and the starting point of all doctrines of the Church. Christology, the study whose object is the Person and work of Christ, remains the solid foundation for the doctrine of the Lord's Supper. "But whom say ye that I am?" is still the fundamental question which confronts the Christian and the Church. The possibility of becoming a Christian, the whole point of Christian teaching and the power of the Church in the world is absolutely dependent upon the answer to this question of Christ. And no less than the same Holy Spirit by whom Peter made his confession of faith in the Person of

Christ shall reveal within us our confession, "Thou art the Christ, the Son of the living God."

The essential element in New Testament Christianity is that it came to determine, in a final way, the Person of Jesus Christ as the Son of God, the Savior of the world. All else is secondary. The Gospels are selective narratives of the Person and work of Jesus Christ, and faith in this historic fact (cf. John 20:31). Christianity is not just the historic fact, but faith in the superhistoric fact, living on in a new experience which it creates. It is justifying faith in a forgiving God through the Cross of Jesus Christ. The disciples and the Gospel writers never considered the figure of Jesus without the corresponding fact of the incarnation, the Cross, the resurrection, the ascension, and the imminent *parousia*. Christianity without faith in the Person of Christ is not Christianity. A faith must have object and content; and in Christianity, it is Christ. Religious dogma or spiritual feeling is not Christianity. Christianity is not a scheme of beautiful precepts or benign charities. Personal faith means much more than a romantic idealism. This is too subjective and does not contain that which makes Christianity Christian. Christianity is faith in Christ, in which is the experience of forgiveness and salvation and a new life which God alone can give.

The Person of Christ is the crux in the issue of Christianity today. The battle is not religion or nonreligion, faith or nonfaith, but answering belief in Christ. This is certainly not proposing an issue, but sharpening the existing issue, in order that it may be explicit and clear for the choice of Christians and the Church. An historical religion like Christianity always faces this issue. Christianity gradually accommodates itself to its environment and is gradually absorbed, forgetting the point from which it started and severing itself from the source from which it is sustained. The subtle danger for Christianity is a religious syncretism which does not bear the marks of Jesus Christ. Our religious world has many moral ideals: relationship of man to man, man to community, and nation to nation; but it forgets the relationship of the guilty soul with God. Society always seeks its righteousness, but a righteousness that is alien to the righteousness of God in Christ. Humanism concerns itself with man's religion, rather than with God's salvation. The first business of Christianity is man's faith in the Person of Christ.

To know Jesus Christ as Lord and Savior, however, does not change the complexity of the Person and the doctrine. We can ever elucidate a doctrine of the Person of Christ; yet a final word ever evades us. He entered the world in the simplicity of human nature, and yet in a mystery of divine nature. With omnipotent power He acted upon man and nature, and yet He suffered Himself to be crucified and buried in an earthen tomb. He had a cosmic concern, and yet a heart that received and loved little children. He had a scathing tongue for the Pharisaical religiosity which pretended to love God, but helping hands for the social misfits and those broken in heart and body. He was the bread of life, and yet He hungered. He was the spring of living water, and yet He asked a woman for a drink. "In the thick of life and love He remained unloved, sympathetic yet aloof, cleaving at once both to man and solitude. He spoke with such power because he loved silence with an almost sacramental idea of human relations, especially the central relation of marriage; yet He avoided for Himself every bond of property, or family; and He cut these bonds when they stood between men and Himself. Full of biting irony upon men, He yet was their healer and Savior."[1] He was King and subject, Ruler and servant, Prince and pauper, God and man.

The nature of the Person of Christ is the perplexing question, even within the Christian community. Generally the teaching of God the Father is received without question. The Christian ideals and ethics are accepted as true, whether they are

[1] Forsyth, P. T., *The Person and Place of Jesus Christ,* (London: Independent Press, 1946), p. 65.

practiced or not. The doctrine of faith is received without serious questioning. Even the institution of the Church is accepted by the social community as a good thing. But the orthodox doctrines of the incarnation of Christ, the divine-human nature of Christ, and the Trinity of God become a stumbling stone to total Christian belief. There is little doubt that a considerable number of sincere Church members, while impressed sufficiently by the figure of the Man of Nazareth, are strangely silent concerning the Person of Christ. This study is designed to relate Christology to the doctrine of Holy Communion by saying that a weak Christological doctrine in the Church will inevitably result in a weak sacramental doctrine. Conversely, a strong belief in the Person of Christ will inevitably result in a strong sacramental doctrine and in a faithful practice of Holy Communion by all who lay claim to Him.

Those who attempt to "schematize" the Person of Christ will be sorely disappointed, for some things are irreducible to proof or logic. The greatest things we believe we cannot comprehend, not only in religion, but in everyday life. Nor is it "irrational" if our statements concerning the Person of Christ appear to be flat contradictions. The greatest realities are often the greatest paradoxes. Be suspicious of a simple doctrine concerning the Person of Christ. It is obviously true that most Christian heresies arose from an oversimplification of the great mysteries of God, an undue emphasis for a rational understanding. It is impossible to find a rational scheme to contain the Person of Christ. In this respect good scientists acknowledge the inadequacy of rationality for reality. Good science recognizes faith as a way of knowledge. In fact, science gives us only method; whereas, faith gives us reality. The old absolute claim of pure logical dogma has not been found equal to the demands of modern life. No dogma is adequate for spiritual reality. Our whole destiny of life is risked upon things that are real and yet uncontained in a rational scheme. Therefore, when we turn to Christianity and see that

God and man seem to exclude each other, when we realize the depth of difference, then we realize the greatness of the Person of Christ who bridges the abysmal chasm in the incarnation as true man and true God.

In a very real sense the Person of Christ can only be known personally. Salvation is essential for any doctrinal approach to Christology. As essential as Christology is for teaching the Person of Christ, yet we really know Him only when our life is hid with Christ in God (cf. Col. 3:3). Only by the saving action which sets us in Christ and assures us of the incredible fact that we are included by God's grace do we "know" Jesus Christ. We know the Person of Christ only as we taste of the love, grace, and mercy of God. The failure to know the Person of Christ is, in the final analysis, a moral failure, a willful refusal to receive Him as a personal Savior (cf. John 7:17). Often this failure is a result of a defective estimate of sin from which He saves. The soteriological basis for our Christology is broader than we sometimes recognize. Personal salvation forms the means whereby we can pursue the doctrine of the Person of Christ. Christ can't be discussed in isolation from His saving work in us. Regardless of our belief concerning the nature and extent of sin and the redemption from sin by Jesus Christ, we can be affirmative about *who* He is by *what* He has *done*. In other words, the Person and work of Christ lend to each other their meaning; and the work of Christ is to "seek and save the lost," and through the Cross.

Christian faith becomes the foundation of Christian theology. Jesus Christ can be *known* only by those who are on *speaking terms* with Him. To all who claim Christ we ask, "In the days of His flesh, did He relate salvation with His teaching and works or with His Person? Did He come to teach about men and ethical principles or to transform men with new power, the power of the Spirit of God?" Who are we to insist that Christ shall qualify according to naturalistic religious standards and human ideals which are brought to

Him from sinful natures? Rather, isn't Christ His own standard, from which all else is judged; isn't He our King, Redeemer, Savior, and Lord? When we come to God in Christ, we confront, not rational conclusions, but personal decision; not facts, but faith; not compromise with our sin and His sinlessness, but a clear choice of His salvation. He is not the champion of the sophisticated dignity of mankind, but the Christ-Savior of man's spiritual wretchedness and moral degradation. Christian scholars recognize that the issue has always been between a rational and a redemptive Christianity. Redemptive Christianity is most reasonable, but not rational. Man always seeks to evade decision by contemplation. Throughout history the Church has almost committed suicide by trying to make itself compatible with natural philosophies and the State. The Church is ever incompatible in the world because it is like "new wine in old skins," "a new patch on an old cloth." The new rends the old, and we as Christians are "new creatures" in an old sinful world. The "Word became flesh" and addresses us in the Person. God breaks into the monologue of sinful society and confronts us in the Person of Christ. Man can be addressed only as a person by a person. Therefore, out of sheer love and grace, God condescended to man in the Person of Christ. God is present in our midst in the Person of the Savior and awaits our personal decision, not our singular or collective deliberations. "Person" means precisely that which we cannot *have* or *possess*, but *love* and *become*.

That the Person of Christ can be known only by those who are in a personal saving relationship with Him is made evident in His earthly ministry. The scribes and Pharisees sought for a sign by which they could determine His Person and authority (cf. Matt. 12:38, 39). Christ refused their proposition, vindicating Himself. They proposed empirical proofs upon the basis of their own perverted presuppositions and for the purpose of their own desires. The Person of God never submitted to this kind of empirical proof. Jesus Christ was in their presence and the vindication was *in* Him, not *about* Him. This is why the Lord in His earthly ministry did not teach about Himself as the Person of God. He did not impose upon His disciples a doctrine of His Person. He was Himself the revelation of the Person of God, not just a prophet teaching about God. We call to mind that questions always indicate the questioner and his presuppositions in the question. Jesus Christ was interested in the questioner, not in the questions that were addressed to Him about Himself. When a person addresses the Absolute it is never to question Him; it is only to praise and adore Him.

Since the Person of Jesus Christ has a historic claim we must, at the beginning of the study, ask the serious question, What kind of certainty can we have about the historical narratives of our Lord? Form criticism says we can't have any accuracy concerning the historic Person of Jesus. This movement has expressed its approach to Jesus as, "Man's knowledge and mastery of the world have advanced to such an extent through science and technology that it is no longer possible for anyone seriously to hold the New Testament view of the world – in fact, there is hardly anyone who does."[2] This type of criticism is totally unacceptable in the Christian faith. It always seems strange that these New Testament scholars should seek to destroy the very thing they are studying! It is like turning out the light by which one is reading, or discarding the map by which one is being directed. Form criticism which destroys the New Testament Scriptures is dangerous heresy. An accurate and reliable narrative of the life of Jesus of Nazareth is contained in the New Testament Gospels.

Christians believe that God, from out of the cosmos, in a particular land, among a select Messianic People, sent forth His Son in the "fullness of time." At this point in history God

[2] Bultmann, Rudolf, *New Testament and Mythology,* trans. Reginald A. Fuller, (London: S.P.C.K., 1960), p. 4.

revealed His love, mercy, and redemption in His only begotten Son, Jesus Christ. In heaven and earth, "Therefore God raised him to the heights and bestowed on him the name above all names, that at the name of Jesus every knee should bow – in heaven, on earth, and in the depths – and every tongue confess, 'Jesus Christ is Lord,' to the glory of God the Father" (Phil. 2:9-11). *Therefore, it seems incredible that God should not have preserved in record, as well as in Life, that for which He took centuries to prepare and fulfill in His Son!* Certainly the same God and Father that is Master of heaven and earth is also Master of the records of His action in Holy Scriptures. The Holy Scriptures are of God! They stand as such.

Revelation and Christian Faith

Christianity is based on revelation. It is only by the revelation of God that we can know God at all. We come to God only through His revelation of Himself through Himself. Even the unbeliever's questions are derived out of the revelation of God in Christ. The questioning of the nature, attributes, and action of God is based upon the nature, attributes, and action of His Person. We assume that we know what the attributes of God are; but, in fact, we know them only through the revelation of God in Christ. We question the love of God, and yet we can only question the love of God through His gift of love – His Son. We contemplate the goodness of God, and yet we can only contemplate goodness because of the goodness of God revealed in Him. We wonder about the mercy of God, and yet mercy is questioned only because we know of mercy in the Lord Jesus Christ. We speak the name God as though we can will and determine its meaning, and yet it is only by His grace that we can even speak the name. In other words, the self-revelation of God in Christ is the basis of our approach to the Person of Christ. As sinful creatures we are helpless to begin the investigation on our own.

The meaning of revelation and its necessity as "a priori" in our Christian faith has been abundantly set forth in our modern Christian theology. The new theology has brought to our attention as never before our utter dependence on the grace of God. In fact this new theology has emphasized the Christ of faith to the extent that the historical Jesus of Nazareth has been overshadowed. The emphasis upon revelation by this new theology is certainly in harmony with our Christian doctrine, and we gladly accept its thrust into the Christian world. At the same time we are not unmindful to discern points of differences between this new theology and our own Christian doctrine. To begin with, we understand as never before that although we can understand our fellow creatures because they are "fellows," we can not begin to understand or know the nature of God because He is God. He is divine; we are human, fallen human beings at that, and there is no common ground of Holy Communion. The sphere or realm of God is entirely above our own. There is not even a point of contact without the Mediator. "Thus knowledge of the real personal God is possible only through a personal self-communication of God through revelation, in which He imparts to us what we ourselves could never know – not even by any attempt to probe the foundations of life, by any self-directed effort or thought – through the communication of His Proper Name, of His secret."[3] The invitation to communion must come from God, through revelation, by the very nature of His being God.

There is no "a priori," no beginning, apart from the revelation of God. Man of himself cannot possibly attain to God, and his attempts are futile and misdirected. The God that man seeks to "design" by his own will and rational powers is a perverted design by the fact that man's will and rational power are sin-perverted in a corrupt world. As Paul said,

[3] Brunner, Emil, *The Mediator,* trans. Olive Wyon, (London: The Lutterworth Press, 1934), p. 211.

"They boast of their wisdom, but they have made fools of themselves, exchanging the splendor of immortal God for an image shaped like mortal man, even for images like birds, beasts, and creeping things" (Rom. 1:22, 23). Since the fall, man is sunk in sin and cannot rise by his own efforts; he is bound by sin and cannot liberate himself. The very nature of sin is to camouflage itself beyond recognition as sin by any who are enmeshed in it. We cannot recognize evil as evil until we are no longer enmeshed in evil. We can only recognize the fall as such when we ourselves have returned to a starting point. Only then are we in truth and there in a position whence we can really *see* the evil. Thus the divine revelation is at the same time a revelation of the Holy God, and of sinful man.

Sin affects not only the spiritual and social aspects of man, but also his rational powers. We are not concerned so much with consideration of the degree of the effect of sin on the rational power of man as with its untrustworthiness as a result of sin. The rational power of sinful man, even a genius, is still infected with a deathly deceptiveness. This very basic deceptiveness is described by Paul, "For we see divine retribution from heaven and falling upon all godless wickedness of men. In their wickedness they are stifling the truth. For all that may be known of God by men lies plain before their eyes, indeed God himself disclosed it to them . . . to the eye of reason . . . but they have refused to honor him as God. . . . Hence all their thinking has ended in futility and their misguided minds are plunged in darkness" (Rom. 1:18-21). It is to this darkness that the light of God has come through Jesus Christ. Darkness cannot of itself generate light; light must come to the darkness: "All that came to be was alive with his life, and that life was the light of men. The light shines on in the dark, and the darkness has never quenched it" (John 1:4, 5). Thus the revelation of God precedes all knowledge of God. Truth about the divine does not proceed from us, but comes to us in the revelation of God in Christ.

Further, sin not only destroys the inner capacities of man, but also sets itself up in a self-will against the will of God in the heart of man. Sinful man in a sense rebels from God, the Creator, and sets up his own domain against the dominion of God. He seeks to be self-sufficient and avoid any acknowledgment of himself as a dependent creature of the Creator. The essence of evil is that it seeks to propagate itself, to continue its kind. It is in this dominion of sinful humanity where revelation is essential to break through, cut the power of sin, and establish a new creation, the Kingdom of God. When the revelation of God in Christ comes and confronts man, he either surrenders to Him, or is offended in Him. The issue in the revelation of the person of Christ has been drawn and there is no neutral ground. "He who is not with me, is against me, and he who does not gather with me scatters" (Matt. 12:30). Therefore, "he alone really confesses his sin who has surrendered the last line of defense, who does not withdraw into himself and take refuge in the depths of his own being . . . with every kind of affirmation of God in us. For he alone really surrenders, he alone declares himself a liar, that God alone may have the truth."[4] This is the necessity and force of revelation of God in Christ in the world. We cannot make an ally of our sinful domain with His New Kingdom; we change citizenships. Man's highest moralism and humanism remain within the sphere of the principalities and powers that have been condemned to death (cf. Col. 1). The revelation comes to reconcile the world, to do for man what man can't do for himself.

The revelation of the Christian faith is understood when contrasted with humanism. Man may aspire and actually climb to the top of Mount Everest, but he is still on earth. A man may be a genius in ideas and a giant in ideals, but this is a matter of *degree*, not *kind*, and he is still in the sphere of sinful humanity. Humanism sets its own standard, which is sinful

[4] Brunner, *op. cit.*, p. 230.

humanity, rather than Almighty God. As is commonly described in theology, humanism is a "monologue"; it is still conversation within the same realm. The very highest forms of philosophies, art, music and ideals are still creaturely. Sinful man continually tends vainly to flatter himself by comparison with fellow creatures, forgetting that his fellow creatures are in the same sinking ship and provide no eternal standard. The most sublime human spirit is still a creature. All the best fruits of humanism remain within the sphere of humanity, and it is this whole sphere that is plunged into sin and death. We recognize that this concept of humanism is from the circle of faith. That only we who lay claim to the new creation have this view of the old creation. However, the fact of sin and death in the old creation is strongly evident, even from a humanistic viewpoint.

God in Christ comes into humanity from without. It is His own Word about Himself, His revelation, based on the fact that He alone is God. The very nature of God demands that He reserve this self-movement to Himself; He is the Creator revealing Himself to His creatures. If it is not His revelation based solely on His self-expression, then it is not revelation. The self-revelation of God in Christ is absolute and, in this sense, is unique from all that is in the sphere of the material and historical. The iron curtain between God and man is thrown down; eternal life has entered the realm of death; the abysmal gulf, which no ethical, religious, humanistic speculation can cross, has been bridged. Jesus Christ has come from God to man, from life to death, from light to darkness, from glory to the form of a servant, that He might redeem and re-create sinful men. Revelation is as important to the Christian faith as the sunrise to the earth; without it man would remain in perpetual darkness. Our belief in revelation is the belief that God Himself is the beginning of everything that begins.

Placing primary emphasis upon the revelation of God in Christ might be objected to as too one-sided. When and how does man respond to the Almighty who reveals Himself on His own terms? We would answer, first of all, that the revelation of God includes His communion with man. In revelation God doesn't just *communicate* with us, He *communes* with us. God's revelation is not the communication of propositions, but the communion of spirits. This is the distinction between the prophets and the Lord Jesus Christ. The prophet was God's mouthpiece, the messenger who delivered the message. He had no choice in the message which was of God. The prophet's word has authority, only because it is not his own, but God's. The message of the prophet was *a* revelation of God, but not *the* revelation. *The* revelation was in the Person of Jesus Christ. Christ does not have a revelation, nor just deliver a message as does a prophet. Christ is Himself the message, the Holy One who is the Word of God. The prophet who carries a revelation is one among many. As a human being he stands upon the same human level, regardless of his divine message. Christ is the "only begotten," the shining, solitary figure in time, in splendid separation from all others, from all else. "No man," they answered, "ever spoke as this man speaks" (John 7:46).

"A true Christology will tell us not simply that God is *like* Christ, but that God was *in* Christ. Thus it will tell us not only about the *nature* of God, but about His *activity*, about what He has done, coming the whole way for our salvation in Jesus Christ; and there is no other way in which the Christian truth about God can be expressed."[5]

The Christian faith is above all else the revealed knowledge of God as one who saves. As far as the world is concerned, the revelation of God in Christ is for the salvation of man, that is, the forgiveness of sins. The revelation of God in Christ was not to answer the universal, the cosmological, or even the social questions, but to answer the ultimate ques-

[5] Baillie, D. M., *God Was In Christ,* (London: Faber and Faber, 1961), pp. 66, 67.

tion, "If a man die shall he live again?" (Job 14:14). The question is answered, "Because I live, ye shall live also" (John 14:19).

The Foundation of Communion

What is the significance of the Person of Christ and revelation to Communion? The deity of Jesus Christ means divine authority and eternal finality. His Person means that the forgiveness of sins through Him is God's forgiveness. Peter preached, "Be it known unto you all . . . that by the name of Jesus Christ of Nazareth, whom ye crucified, whom God raised from the dead . . . is become the head of the corner. Neither is there salvation in any other; for there is none other name under heaven given among men, whereby we must be saved" (Acts 4:10-12). The Apostle Paul declared, "Wherefore God also hath highly exalted him, and given him a name which is above every name: That at the name of Jesus every knee should bow, of things in heaven, and things in earth, and things under the earth" (Phil. 2:9, 10). The finality of authority in this forgiveness is that He is the Person of God. It is not simply that He is sinless and shows perfect love that we have assurance with God, for this is speculation by human standards. Rather it is God in Christ who says, "Thy sins be forgiven thee." The point of His divine nature is not merely that He was come to reveal something, some divine secret whereby we can come to a rational understanding of God, but that we might receive the perfect forgiveness that communion with God demands. What God demands of us He provides in Himself. If Christ were merely human then He would be merely an example toward which we strive, in frustration and defeat, rather than the source of life. It is His divine nature that makes the Cross a divine atonement. Because He is the Son of God the Cross is the means of man's reconciliation to God. He is the way of man to God.

Revelation means that God has come to us in the flesh as

the whole to the sick, as new to the old, as the Sinless One to sinners, that the divine bridge may be anchored on both sides. His tabernacling in the flesh was not to incorporate the best in man, his intellectual systems. On the contrary, God's revelation shatters all vain hopes of man in himself. The coming of God in the incarnation was not like a metaphysical demigod uniting God and humanity. The revelation of the Person of Christ first of all contrasted God and man, then provided the way for man to be re-created out of the old creation of sin and death. The revelation of the Person of Christ is not for a mere show of God to man, but for the regeneration of man. The significance of the revelation is that it is *from* God *to* man, that by grace through faith man can return to God and his "imago dei."

The Person of Christ is also significant in that it is the everlasting love of God seeking sinners, "We love Him because He first loved us." In the divine nature of Christ is the One who is Himself God, One who does not seek God as humanity seeks. Christ as the Son of God does not tremble before the judgment of God, but is the One who judges! The Person of Christ is not seeking to enter the eternal Kingdom of God, but is the One who brings in the Kingdom. He is the One who descended to earth before ascending to heaven. He brings us to God because He is from God, He is of the Godhead. Anyone, or any teaching, that weakens or destroys the teaching of the Person of Christ, weakens and destroys the very source of Holy Communion. We believe in the divine nature of Christ for by it we have apprehended the very source of life, "Whosoever drinketh of the water that I shall give him shall never thirst; but the water that I shall give him shall be in him a well of water springing up into everlasting life" (John 4:14).

Holy Communion is rooted in the Person of Christ and is concerned with the *who* He is rather than the *how*. The New Testament Scriptures and the early Church Fathers interpreted the nature of Christ by His *being*, rather than by His physical or material nature. When a person allows a materialistic metaphysic to be the center of his attention concerning the Person of Christ it is the self-incriminating evidence that he is trying to understand the Creator by creaturely methods, an impossibility. The difference between the Son of Man and sinful men is not *degree*, but *kind*. He is Himself God revealed, and in the presence of the Person of the Godhead a metaphysical explanation is absurd. In the presence of God in Christ our only choice is confession, confession of belief, "My Lord and my God."

The divine nature of Christ means that the veil of the temple could be rent and Holy Communion established. No earthly priest could follow the longing of his soul, or the soul of his people, and cross over and ascend unto God. The agonizing spots of sin remained, regardless of religious exercise, "For it is not possible that the blood of bulls and of goats should take away sins. Wherefore when He came into the world . . . after he hath offered one sacrifice for sins for ever, sat down on the right hand of God. For by one offering he hath perfected for ever them that are sanctified" (Heb. 10:2, 12, 14). Only the Person of Christ, in the human sphere, could enact the eternal sacrifice for sins. Only He who is sinless could provide the eternal sacrifice for sins. Only He who is sinless could atone for sin, and sinlessness demands divine nature. Thus our Great High Priest of Holy Communion can only be absolutely of God Himself, and in this sense differs from all others that are begotten in human history. The divine nature of Christ means the coming of God in Christ in an incomprehensible self-movement. Holy Communion symbolizes that the veil is rent, the wall is broken down, the bridge has been made in the God-Man. Rejoice, and be glad, for through Him our enmity to God has been reconciled, our sins have been redeemed, our death has been defeated and we receive His gift of eternal life!

The Person of Christ makes intelligible the resurrection. Only the One with divine power could say, "No man taketh it from me, but I lay it down of myself, I have power to lay it down, and I have power to take it again" (John 10:18). His earthly ministry evidenced the transcendent nature of His being only faintly, (cf. Transfiguration, Mark 9), but in the resurrection the full meaning of His oneness with God was realized. The Apostles in the book of Acts, spoke repeatedly of the Resurrected One, the Lord Jesus Christ. The good news of Christ permeated every practice of Holy Communion in the early Church with exuberance. The last enemy of man, death, had been conquered. The divine nature of Christ in the power of the resurrection dispels forever the "shadowing sheol," and brings all who are in Him into the glory of His Father, now *Our Father.*

The proclamation of the resurrection in Holy Communion would be worthless, worse than worthless, "And if Christ be not risen, then is our preaching vain, and your faith is also vain . . . and we are of all men most miserable" (I Cor. 15: 17-19), if we did not believe in the deity of Christ. The resurrection of Christ is differentiated from all imaginable parallels by its sequel. Its power is affirmed in the life of the believer and the life of the Church. The sovereign power of His risen life can have no successor because He is sovereign. He alone is the Son of God, the Savior of the world.

Jesus Christ is the "only begotten Son." He is unique from us in His very nature, in His divine nature. The very priniciple is that He is Creator, in contrast to our creatureliness. He comes to us in history from beyond history, as the self-expression of God. The Person of Christ is supremely significant therefore, that in His divine revelation there is God's authority, God's forgiveness of sins, God's justification, and God's gift of life.

The foundation of Holy Communion is the Person of Christ in the revelation of God. All that follows in this study of Communion has bearing and value as it is related to the revelation in Christ. Neither the ecclesiology of the church nor the subjectivism of the Christian is the foundation of Holy

Communion. Christians are prone to accept notions and ideas of God which arise out of the commonplace, rather than the revelation of God Himself, in the language of the Word. The term "god" has always been a slippery word meaning many things to many people. Through the revelation of Christ the unknown became known, the invisible became visible, the inconceivable became apprehensible. The meaningful practice of Holy Communion is staked upon the Person of Christ. The invitation to Holy Communion is a divine appointment.

2

The Historic Setting

A STRONG BELIEF IN THE REVELATION OF GOD IN CHRIST DEmands a careful consideration of the historic Christ event. The belief that the Lamb of God was slain before the foundation of the world does not erase Bethlehem, Jerusalem and Calvary from history. Jerusalem is the historic center of Christ's redemptive activity. Christ had a divine appointment with the Father at Jerusalem in the days of His flesh.

Jerusalem and Religious Feasts

The city of Jerusalem is the historic setting of the Last Supper. Jerusalem is the heart of the people of Israel. The great prophet Isaiah speaks of Jerusalem, "Many people shall go and say, come ye, and let us go up to the mountain of Jehovah, to the house of the God of Jacob; and he will teach us of his ways, and we will walk in his paths, for out of Zion shall go forth the law, and the word of Jehovah from Jerusalem" (Isa. 2:3). Jerusalem is shrouded in memories of the past and hopes of the future.

The heart of Jerusalem was the temple. The pilgrims came to the religious celebration, the feast of the Passover, and beholding the beauty of their religious home they sang for joy (Ps. 122). "Terrace upon terrace its courts rose, till high above the city, within the enclosure of marble cloisters, cedar-roofed and richly ornamented, the temple itself stood out a mass of snowy marble and of gold, glittering in the sunlight against the half-encircling green background of Olivet."[1] This is the temple that Herod began to build in 22 B.C. and continued until the time of the Lord, the same temple from which Jesus spoke the words, "Destroy this temple, and in three days I will raise it up." They said, "It has taken forty-six years to build this temple" (John 2:19, 20).

The feast of the Passover was one of the three religious feasts to which every loyal Israelite came. The religious pilgrims from all parts of the land formed pilgrimages and wended their ways to Jerusalem. The feast of Passover and the feast of Unleavened Bread, commonly called simply "Passover," were special feasts, joyous occasions. The Passover was the season when the deadness of winter changed into the freshness of spring, when the planted seeds were born into a new harvest. This is the natural setting for the sacrificing death of Christ and the resurrection of Christ.

The preparation for the feast began many weeks before the Passover. One of the orders for preparation was the whitewashing of the tombs and sepulchers. The ancient cemeteries were outside the cities, close beside the ways, and were whitewashed to warn the people not to touch them – an act making them unclean for the feast. The preparation of whitewashing is probably what Jesus referred to when he said, "Alas for you, lawyers and Pharisees, hypocrites! You are like tombs covered with whitewash; they look well from out-

[1] Edersheim, Alfred, *The Temple,* (London: James Clark, 1959), p. 28.

side, but inside they are full of dead men's bones and of all kinds of filth" (Matt. 23:27).

The number of religious pilgrims that came to Jerusalem for the feasts is difficult to estimate. Josephus recorded 256,500 as the number of lambs slain one year.[2] If there was a minimum of ten persons for every lamb, which was the number required by the law, it would indicate approximately two and a half million people present for the Passover.

The upper room where the disciples prepared and the Lord held his Last Supper remains hidden in the past. Jesus instructed His disciples, "Go to a certain man in the city, and tell him, 'The Master says, My appointed time is near; I am to keep Passover with my disciples at your house'" (Matt. 26:18). The obvious understanding from the words, "The Master says," is that the home was that of a friend, a follower of the Master." "When we remember the teeming multitude in the very small city at this feast time, it is rather evident that this private room was reserved for the Master for this very special gathering. The upper room was undoubtedly in a large house, one that was prepared and given to the Visitor whom it was desired to honor."[3]

The Last Supper in the upper room is, without question, in the setting of the feast of the Passover, when the hearts of the people of God turned to remember the deliverance of the past from the bondage of Egypt and to remember the promises of the prophets concerning the deliverance of the future. Approximately twenty times in the Gospels the Passover season is given as the setting for the Last Supper. The ministry and life of the Lord inevitably led to Jerusalem and the Cross, "He set his face resolutely towards Jerusalem" (Luke 9:51). The Lord charged His disciples to be silent concerning His signs in His early ministry, but consented to the acclamations,

[2] Josephus, *Jew Wars,* Vol. VI,9.3., 14.3.

[3] Bouquet, A. C., *Everyday Life in New Testament Times,* (London: Batsford, 1954), p. 30.

"Hosanna! blessed is he that cometh in the name of the Lord" (Mark 11:9) in the last days of His ministry in the flesh. The Son of God has come to be the Lamb of God, the Suffering Servant of Israel and the world.

Christ anxiously awaited His passion: "How I have longed to eat *this* Passover with you before my death" (Luke 22: 15). Christ had celebrated other Passovers in Jerusalem (John 2:13; 6:4), but this was the one ordained of God "to lay down His life" (John 10:15, 17). Following His disclosure at Caesarea Philippi that He was the Christ, the Son of the living God, each day was lived with added reverence. Passovers themselves were the high points of the Jewish year, but this Passover was to be the high point of history.

The Identification of the Last Supper

The identification of the Last Supper has always been a problem for serious Bible students. The problem simply stated is that the Synoptic accounts describe the Last Supper in the language of a Passover meal; whereas, the Johannine account describes it as taking place on the "day of preparation." Mark so clearly indicates the Passover that only this day can be meant by him: "Now on the first day of Unleavened Bread, *when the Passover lambs were being slaughtered*, his disciples said to him, 'Where would you like us to go and prepare for you Passover supper.' Then the disciples went off, and when they came into the city they found everything just as he told them. So they prepared for the Passover. In the evening he came to the house with the twelve. As they ate at supper Jesus said. . . . During the supper he took bread, and having said the blessing he broke it and gave it to them . . ." (Mark 14:12, 16, 17, 18, 22). Matthew and Luke also give this same Passover meal setting for the Last Supper. According to these Synoptic accounts the sacrificing of the paschal animals took place in the afternoon of Nisan 14, and in the evening began Nisan 15 at which time Jesus and His disciples went to the upper room and celebrated the Passover meal as the Last Supper.

The Gospel of John, however, seems to differ in chronology from the Synoptic Gospels by identifying the Last Supper as taking place on the "day of preparation" (John 13:1; 18:28; 19:14, 31, 42) before the Passover meal: "From Caiaphas Jesus was led into the Governor's headquarters. It was now early morning, and the Jews themselves stayed outside the headquarters to avoid defilement, so that they could eat the Passover meal" (John 18:28).

The Gospel of Mark leads some Bible scholars to believe that the Last Supper was a Passover meal held on Nisan 15.[4] The reasons set forth are that the Last Supper received particular preparation and was held at night in Jerusalem as prescribed by the law for the Passover meal (Exod. 12:18). The disciples were present at the Last Supper in recumbent position, which was traditional for free men, in contrast to the manner of the standing of slaves. Both the Egyptian and permanent Passover required a definite number of participants which requirement was fulfilled by the twelve disciples with the Lord. That the courses of the Passover mean cups of blessing,[5] loaf breaking, and main meal is evident in the Gospel accounts. The service of washing and cleansing is evidenced in the Last Supper (John 13). The Passover prayers and blessings seem to fit the sayings of the Lord. The singing of the Passover hymn could well be the hymn singing recorded in the Gospels. Following the Supper the Lord and His disciples remained in the Jerusalem district, the garden of Gethsemane, for the Passover celebration.

The similarity of the Last Supper to the Passover meal celebration is remarkable. However, the activities of the Lord in that last night which deny its being a Passover cele-

[4] Cf. Higgins, J. G., *The Lord's Supper in the New Testament,* (London: SCM, 1960), Jeremiah, J., *The Eucharistic Words of Jesus,* (Oxford: Basil Blackwell), 1955.

[5] Four cups of red wine are required: Mishnah, Pesahim 109.9.

bration are also noteworthy. There is no mention of the paschal lamb; a common cup is used instead of individual cups which were customary for the Passover meal; His enemies were seeking to avoid arresting Him during the feast (Mark 14:2); and it is highly unlikely that the session of the Sanhedrin and the condemnation of Jesus to crucifixion would occur on the night of Passover. Therefore, it becomes unreasonable to conclude that the Last Supper was a Passover meal.

The language of the Gospel of John concerning the Last Supper leads many to believe that the Last Supper was not the Passover meal, but simply a religious meal held on Nisan 14, perhaps a Jewish Chaburah. The form of the Jewish Chaburah with which Jesus would have been familiar can be outlined as follows:[6] (1) preliminary course of relishes over which each guest would say a blessing; (2) reclining of guest for the formal meal which began with handwashing and blessing; (3) the formal meal then beginning with the leader taking bread, breaking it as he said, "Blessed be Thou, O Lord our God, King of the Universe, who bringest forth bread from earth," following the prayer of blessing he himself eating and distributing to each one present. As each course was served the leader would offer the blessing; (4) at the close of the meal hands being washed again; (5) the final prayer of benediction; and (6) at special occasions not uncommonly the final blessing given over a special cup of wine. The final prayer included thanksgiving for the providential supplying of food, for mercy on Israel in history, for the promised land, for the exodus, and for the covenant. There was also the singing of a hymn at a Chaburah.

There is striking harmony between this form of Chaburah and the Last Supper as accounted in the Gospels. The procedure at the Last Supper includes, first of all, the preliminary relishes with a cup of wine where Jesus made His prayer-

[6] **Mishnah, Berakoth.**

vow: "For I tell you, never again shall I eat it until the time when it finds its fulfillment in the kingdom of God" (Luke 22:16). Then comes the feet-washing service in which Jesus washes the disciples' feet (John 13:1-17). The formal supper then begins with Jesus' grace over the broken bread, "This is my body. Do this in remembrance of me" (Luke 22:19). Table conversation led by the Lord includes the subjects of the preparation of the future, the Comforter, their relationship to Him as the branches to the vine, and the activity of the Holy Spirit in the world (John 14:15, 16). The final cup of blessing is passed and shared by all, at which time He says, "This cup is the new covenant in my blood which will be poured out for many. Do this in remembrance of me" (Mark 14:24; Luke 22:19). After singing the Passover hymn, they went out to the Mount of Olives (Mark 14:26)!

The Last Supper seems to harmonize with a Jewish Chaburah. However, we could not positively identify the Last Supper with a Chaburah simply on the basis of similarity and association. The religious meal was a well-established custom in Judaism, and it is a remarkable fact that our Lord participated in many meal fellowships, particularly with His chosen band of disciples. However, we do not need to identify the Last Supper with Jewish social customs to validate it as the Lord's Supper. The Last Supper is more than a semi-religious meal held on a Sabbath, on feast days, or on "days of preparation." The Supper of our Lord is a "covenant" meal instituting Himself as the Lamb of God.

We must recognize the transforming power of Jesus Christ to take any common meal and transform it to a sacred and holy sacrament. Christ's words, "What I am doing you do not know now, but afterward you will understand," illustrate that this meal was the institution of the new. An old form was given new and sacred meaning; old words were charged with eternal significance, and an Old Covenant was recreated into a New Covenant by the authority and power of the Son of God, and by the sacrificial act of Jesus Christ on the Cross.

Of these things we are certain; therefore, the obscurity of its identification can remain in the shadow of the last night. The Last Supper is made the Lord's Supper, not by traditional association, but by the power and Person of the Lord Himself!

The terms, "days of preparation," and "Passover," as designating the time of the Last Supper have perplexed Bible students through the centuries. And although many profound Bible scholars have proposed varied answers, it is still an open question today. We are not presuming to give the final answer relative to the problem of the time of the Last Supper. The problem is caused in part by some peculiar traditions and circumstances surrounding the Jewish Passover. One circumstance to be noted is that there was the "Egyptian" Passover and the "permanent" Passover.[7] These two Passover traditions wrought many changes in religious laws over the years. An example of a change is the position of the guests at the feast: the Egyptian Passover was observed with shoes on, standing; whereas the permanent Passover was eaten with shoes off, reclining. Another circumstance which complicates the problem of identifying the Last Supper is that the Passover and the feast of Unleavened Bread were two distinct festivals under the one term "Passover." The feast of Unleavened Bread was an agricultural feast, celebrating the beginning of the barley harvest. The Passover, from "Persach," which means to "step over," was the animal-offering feast, celebrating the sacrificial deliverance of the Israelites from their bondage in Egypt. The feast of Passover itself took place on the fifteenth of Nisan; the feast of Unleavened Bread commenced on the next day and lasted for seven days.[8] Thus the preparation and practice of the Passover feast being combined with the preparation and practice of the feast of Unleavened Bread caused complicated religious laws. The com-

[7] Exodus 12, Mishnah, Pes. 9.5.
[8] Edersheim, *op. cit.*, pp. 181-182.

plicated Passover preparation became more involved when it fell on a Sabbath with all its rules and practices. This specific preparation for the Sabbath is referred to by Mark in relation to the burial of Jesus: "By this time evening had come; and as it was preparation-day, that is, the day before the sabbath . . ." (Mark 15:42). This reference is to the preparation for the Sabbath as Sabbath, not specifically to preparation for the Passover Sabbath, or to feast of Unleavened Bread Sabbath.[9] These are but a few of the circumstances which make the identification of the Last Supper in the Gospels most difficult, if not impossible. In a word, we can't speak with finality concerning the laws and practices of Judaism in the lifetime of our Lord, for we are removed not only by centuries of time, but also by the intricate realm of laws which are foreign to our life and faith.

It is important, however, not to overemphasize the differences between the fourth Gospel and the Synoptics. The term "synoptic," as applied to the first three Gospels, tends to imply that they are a unity in contrast to the Gospel of John. This is misleading, for there are important differences between one Synoptic Gospel and another, as between them and the fourth Gospel. The Gospel writers were inspired to use the traditions and teachings in the forms and words in which these had come to them; at the same time they believed it important, by selected omissions, to place them in a setting which each evangelist thought needed emphasizing at the time when he was writing, and to the people or churches for which he was writing.[10] John uses distinct phraseology for his distinct writing, not to separate it from the preceding Gospels, but to supplement and interpret them.

The similarity of the Gospel accounts of the eve of crucifixion is most evident. All the Gospels and Paul agree that the

[9] De Vaux, *op. cit.*, pp. 316ff.

[10] Cf. Lightfoot, R. H., *St. John's Gospel,* (Oxford: Clarendon Press, 1956), p. 28.

Last Supper took place in the evening and extended into the night (Mark 14:17; Matt. 26:20; Mark 14:30; John 13:30; I Cor. 11:23). All four Gospels reckon that the day on which Christ was crucified was a Friday (Mark 15:42; Matt. 27:62; Luke 23:54; John 19:31, 42). Thus, from the eve of Thursday to the eve of Friday, the Last Supper, Gethsemane, arrest, trial, crucifixion and burial, all occurred. Also the chronology of the fourth Gospel harmonizes with the Synoptics in many other places: John gives the Passover feast as the setting of the Last Supper (John 13:1-3); the betrayal scene recorded in the Synoptics is also reckoned in John (John 13:18); and the "midnight" walk of the Lord is recorded in both John and Mark (John 18:1; Mark 14:26ff.). It is important to remember that the accounts of the Last Supper in all the Gospels are but the very briefest descriptions of all that occurred in that historic night. The event and its significance are the purpose of the Gospel writers, and this they have fulfilled in the choicest of words. Each word is a gem, filled with the rich mercy of God, in Jesus the Christ.

The Climatic Fellowship

Although the historic identity of the Last Supper with either the Passover or a particular Jewish supper cannot be ascertained, yet the clear points in the setting of the Lord's Supper can be established. The setting of the Lord's Supper is composed of the antecedents which together form the background and give it meaning. Perhaps this is the reason why the identity of the Supper with either the Passover meal or another single type of supper is hidden from sacred history. For if the Last Supper were identified with a single type of Jewish meal, it would limit the meaning of the Lord's Supper in the total concept of Holy Communion.

One of the antecedents of the Lord's Supper is undoubtedly the Passover festival. Although the Supper can't be identified with the feast, yet it is definitely to be viewed against the background of the feast of Passover. The Passover preparations were made; pilgrims were present; and everyone was aware of the presence and meaning of the feast. The Passover ideas must inevitably have been in the mind both of Jesus and of His disciples. The presence of the sacrificial lambs in Jerusalem certainly provides a setting for the "Lamb of God." Whether or not it was a Passover meal, Jesus inaugurated the New Covenant in the breaking of bread and the distribution of the cup which was common to the religious life of His disciples.

We must also take into account the concept of bonded friendship in the "Love-meals." The New Testament is filled with a series of meals which the Lord ate together with His disciples; in fact, He did so to the extent that His enemies called Him, "a glutton and a drunkard" (Luke 7:34). The Jewish Chaburahs included the breaking of bread, the cups of blessing, and the special prayers. Therefore, the influence of these "friendship meals" of the Lord and His disciples cannot be excluded from the Lord's Supper and the "Agape" of the early Church, and in the triune Holy Communion.

The whole historical life and teaching of Christ give meaning to the Lord's Supper. The feeding of the multitudes, the four and the five thousand, and the eating with publicans and sinners are included in the primary considerations of the Supper. The various parables of Jesus, such as the Wedding Feast (Matt. 22:1-14), contribute to the meaning and interpretation of the Lord's Supper. He also spoke of the great Messianic meal of the future when the guests would come from the east and west and sit down together with Abraham, Isaac, and Jacob in the Kingdom of God (Matt. 8:11). The parable of the Ten Virgins anticipates the marriage supper of the Church, as the Bride, to Christ (Matt. 25:1-13). In Jesus' teaching and saving redemption the excommunicated and lost sheep from the house of Israel are compelled to come in and fill the house and partake of the supper prepared. All of these parables and teachings are vital in establishing the real setting of the Lord's Supper and dare not be neglected in our interpretation of the Holy Communion. Thus the richness and fulness of the meaning of the Lord's Supper are based on all these antecedents, rather than on one historical supper.

The antecedents of the Lord's Supper must be added to another significant fact, the post-resurrection appearances and meals of the Lord with His disciples. On Easter Day the two disciples of Emmaus were first of all taught the Scriptures by Christ concerning Himself. "And when he had sat down with them at table, he took bread and said the blessing, he broke the bread, and offered it to them. Then their eyes were opened, and they recognized him" (Luke 24:30, 31). On Easter evening in an upper room, probably the same upper room where the Supper was held a few nights previously, the Lord appeared to His disciples where He ate of their meal. The Lord's breakfast with His disciples at the lake-side is another post-resurrection experience which stamped its impression on the hearts of the disciples (John 21:1-17). The resurrection undoubtedly entered into the formation of the character of the Lord's Supper as practiced by the disciples and the Church. Neither the Passover meal nor the historical supper could have provided the "resurrection spirit" and exuberance that is evidenced in the record of the early Church in Acts. Thus the Lord's Supper enshrines not only the historical Supper before the crucifixion, but also the celebration of the resurrection.

The influence of the resurrection on the Lord's Supper is evidenced in the fact that it was practiced on the Lord's Day, Easter Day, in the early Church. Even persecution and the sentence of death did not stop the celebration of Holy Communion in the Church, for it was filled with the sense of victory in the resurrected Christ.

Therefore, to approach a theological interpretation of the Holy Communion we must take into account the Old Covenant feast of the Passover, the Synoptic accounts, the Jewish religious meals, the Johannine Gospel, the teachings of Christ, the post-resurrection appearances, the tradition of the early

Church in the Pauline accounts, and the practice of the breaking of bread as reflected in the Acts of the Apostles. The elucidation of the Lord's Supper must also include the teaching of the sacrificial act of Christ in the book of Hebrews. The setting of the triune Holy Communion is nothing less than all that God has revealed, and all that Christ has fulfilled in incarnation, crucifixion, resurrection, and ascension.

The fellowship during that last night in the upper room had a divine dimension because God was there, in the incarnate Christ. Although Trinity is nowhere stated in the New Testament, it is everywhere implied. The New Testament makes no clear distinction between God's presence with us, Christ dwelling in us, and the Holy Spirit filling us. These are not three distinct experiences, but one common experience in the full experience of the Christian. This does not mean that there is no distinction, for the incarnation of Christ effected an eternal distinction. However, the believer's experience is one, being solely dependent upon God. "The work of the Son of God includes the work of the Father as its presupposition and the work of the Holy Spirit as its consequence. In a sense, the Person of the Father is the source of life; the Holy Spirit is the strength of life; and the Person of the Son is the way upon which we find ourselves in eternal life. From that vantage we may review the entire fullness of the acts of God."[11] Just as the Trinity of God is three-in-one, so the triune Holy Communion is three-in-one. Just as the actions of the Father, Son and Holy Spirit are inseparable and yet distinguishable, so the action of the Pedilavium, Agape, and Eucharist are inseparable and yet distinguishable. The triune Holy Communion is the most perfect expression of the action and communion of the Trinity of God. The climactic fellowship of the historic upper room results in the Pedilavium, Agape, and Eucharist, to which we turn our attention in the next three chapters.

[11] Barth, Karl, *Dogmatics in Outline,* trans. G. T. Thomson, (London: SCM Press, 1949), p. 71.

3

The Pedilavium

* *Pedilavium,* from *ped* meaning "foot," plus *lavere* meaning "wash," compounded to mean the "Ceremonial Washing of Feet." It is also spelled *pediluvium,* a foot-bath; and *pedilauium.*

HENRY SLOANE COFFIN ONCE ASKED A GROUP OF CHINESE pastors in an interior town what it was in Christ that most impressed them. None of them mentioned the accounts of any miracle. Chinese mythology could outdo the miracles recorded on Gospel pages. Various replies were given, when one elderly man said, "His washing His disciples' feet," and sudden general consensus showed that this incident was peculiarly appealing to them. That a revered teacher would overstep the lines of class and position and take a slave's place was an impressive moral miracle.[1] The bending down of God to man in the Suffering Savior is the signal truth of Christianity.

[1] Wallis, Charles I., *The Table of the Lord,* (New York: Harper and Brothers, 1958), p. 142.

Prerequisite to Communion

The Psalmist asks and answers a vital question of "Holy" communing with the almighty God. "The earth is the Lord's, and the fulness thereof; the world, and they that dwell therein; For he hath founded it upon the seas, and established it upon the floods. Who shall ascend into the hill of the Lord? or who shall stand in his holy place? He that hath clean hands, and a pure heart; who hath not lifted up his soul unto vanity, nor sworn deceitfully. He shall receive the blessing from the Lord, and righteousness from the God of his salvation" (Ps. 24:1-5). The Psalmist begins by affirming that the whole cosmos belongs to God. He is the Creator and Keeper of the world, the world of nature and humanity. It is His in a sense somewhat similar to our right of property, by the efforts of His hands. Because of His complete holy dominion over the fullness of the cosmos, "who dare ascend into the hill of the Lord?" Who is worthy to go before this living God, to stand in His Holy Place? Who dares presume to be worthy to come before the presence of the Lord? Who has the spiritual qualifications prerequisite to His friendship, to communing with the living Holy God? The Psalmist answers his own question. Only "He that hath clean hands . . ." shall commune with God. The answer is substantially the same as in Holy Communion: only he shall really have "Holy Communion" with God who has been made spiritually clean. In the Pedilavium God prepares the communer for his encounter with Himself. To presume to go before the Holy God without proper preparation is the height of human egotism. As God provided the laver as the symbolic cleansing prerequisite to the priests entering the Holy of Holies in the Old Covenant, so He has provided the Pedilavium as the symbolic cleansing prerequisite to believers entering into Holy Communion in the New Covenant. The separating veil into the very presence of God was rent in twain at the time of the Cross. Let all prepare to come before His presence.

Preparation for Holy Communion means far more than the setting of tables, the filling of cups, and the baking of bread. In St. Paul's writing to the Corinthian Christians we learn of a definite spiritual preparation necessary before an effectual Holy Communion, "A man must test (scrutinize, trial) himself, before eating his share of bread and drinking from the cup" (I Cor. 11:28). This is not just a kindly "take-it-or-leave it" admonition, but a stern warning, "For he who eats and drinks eats and drinks judgment on himself if he does not discern the Body" (I Cor. 11:29). At the center of this inward scrutiny for Holy Communion is conscience. Conscience is not acquired by either secular or spiritual education, but is born with us, is natural to us, and is retained by the soul of every human being. It is given by God as the guardian of our souls. It stands guard at the gates of our thoughts and actions, whereby nothing is done in secret, and brings to our attention the sin that destroys or the righteousness that brings new life. If it were not for conscience our souls would be exposed to the world without our even knowing it. When God gave man the free will to choose, He also gave him conscience to effect responsibility in his choices.

Conscience is related to the mind, to this capacity of man which collects, classifies, and comprehends facts. It is in the capacity of the mind that codes are learned and established upon which our conscience cries either "guilty" or "not guilty." Knowledge precedes, not conscience, but the action of conscience. Thus conscience can never affect the judgments of God until the laws of God are established in the person. Immediately some will jump to the conclusion that those who have not been formally taught the laws of God cannot be held guilty or responsible for their thoughts and actions; others will suggest that the laws of God are interpreted in many ways by various peoples making it impossible for the Christian concept of conscience to operate justly. However, the moral and social laws of God are established in all mankind from his very creation in the image of God, and are the basis of his judging conscience. Paul relates this truth to the Roman Christians, "For all that may be known of God by man lies plain before their eyes; indeed God Himself has disclosed it to them. His invisible attributes, that is to say his everlasting power and deity, have been visible, ever since the world began, to the eye of reason, in the things he has made. There is therefore no possible defense for their conduct; knowing God . . ." (Rom. 1:19, 20). In *Huckleberry Finn* Mark Twain stated the same truth in these words, "The moral sense may take up more room in us than all our insides put together." There is a "true light, which lighteth every man." And when a man is perfectly honest he will admit by this inner light what is right and what is wrong. Barth writes, "It is in the light of Jesus Christ that darkness as such is revealed and that consequently it becomes clear in what sin consists."[2] Because the basic laws of God are established in every man, as a part of his natural birth, the power of conscience affects just judgment within every man. Therefore, when Paul declares, "For all alike have sinned and are deprived of the divine splendour" (Rom. 3:23) every hearing soul knows what it means.

What is the effect of conscience in man? When man sins there is the feeling of guilt; if the sin is exceedingly shameful, then the action of the conscience is heavy with fear, guilt, and condemnation. But when man thinks and acts honestly, godly, and justly, then his conscience is at peace. Thus conscience is always active, either condemning or commending man. Since conscience operates within man, its effects are masked and show only a fraction of its feelings on the surface of man. However, the judgment of man's conscience is known in a definite way to himself, and fully to

[2] Barth, Karl, *Church Dogmatics,* trans. by G. W. Bromiley, (Edinburgh: T. & T. Clark, 1956), IV, 1, pp. 123f.

God. Of course wicked men can sin to the extent of hardening conscience, putting it in cold storage, whereby there is little or no feeling of guilt. However, sinful man can never eradicate fear, or a certain final dread of death. When men have turned all light in their lives to darkness, there is blind guilt and fear, but this does not disprove the fact of conscience any more than one rotten, red apple proves all red apples rotten. "There comes a time when the soul will leave the body, but there will never come a time when the conscience will leave the soul."[3]

In the study of Holy Communion what is the significance of this conscience? First of all, that the Christian is not exempt from sins: "We know that the law is spiritual; but I am not; I am unspiritual, the purchased slave of sin. I do not even acknowledge my own actions as mine, for what I want to do, but what I detest. . . . The good which I want to do, I fail to do; but what I do is the wrong which is against my will; and if what I do is against my will, clearly it is no longer I who am the agent, but sin that has its lodging in me" (Rom. 7:14, 15, 19, 20). Therefore, because even as genuine Christians we are prone to sin, our consciences must deal with our own sins as well as our righteousness in Christ. When we sin we weaken our faith in God, begin to doubt His mercy, and bring guilt to our souls. The peace we have with God through justifying faith is pushed into the background of our souls by the struggle between the "spiritual and natural" in our lives. Our first love tends to grow cold and we develop cataracts on our spiritual sight. Sin has the nature of hiding itself within those who sin, of disguising itself in other forms, even in the forms of religion. Thus there is the pressing need within the Christian's life of reaffirming faith, renewing love, and recleansing the heart, which is the dwelling place of the Holy Spirit. The health of our souls and our

[3] Bruce, Robert, *The Mystery of the Lord's Supper,* trans. by T. F. Torrance (Edinburgh: Clarke, 1958), p. 147.

lives depends upon this cleansing from sin and communion with God. Sin does not remain isolated, but tends to become a chain of sins. The greater the sin the greater the one that follows. Thus when we sin we must hurry to the throne of grace, to the fount of mercy, to the arms of the forgiving Father. If we do not flee evil and find the forgiveness of God continually, our consciences become burdened with guilt to the point of mental breakdown. As a Scottish preacher many years ago said, "My meaning is this: No soul can be at peace with God or have any fellowship with the Lord, without in some measure being sanctified and made holy. For God cannot make His residence in a soul that is always a stinking dunghill, and therefore of necessity it must be sanctified. One corner or other of the soul must be made so clean that the Lord of heaven, by His Holy Spirit, may make His residence in it."[4]

The sin in a man's heart has many expressions. The mature Christian knows that when a person tries to rationalize evil, or incessantly speaks about another person's sin, or is sarcastic about goodness in another person's life, or criticizes the Church, or makes light of old standards of morality, he is simply expressing his own guilty conscience. A guilty man speaks loudly to cover his screaming conscience. Sin is not only a Christian concept, but a psychological truth. Sin is like an infectious germ or like a rusty nail in the sole of a child's foot. The body may look normal externally, may even grow good flesh over the rusty nail, but the source of infection continues. The infection not only lives, but grows if not completely removed and cleansed with pure antiseptics. Likewise, when a man commits sin he attempts to rationalize it, to insulate it, and put it out of his immediate memory. But the guilt of sin remains in his conscience; the infection spreads, until the man either turns to God for forgiveness, or returns to his own ends like Judas. Many believe that society's num-

[4] Bruce, *op. cit.*, p. 153.

ber-one health problem, mental disorder and nervous breakdown, is largely the result of unforgiven guilty conscience.[5] Or if the person is physically strong enough to avert breakdown, the bright color of life fades into a drab gray, or the deep joy of life changes into a monotonous existence. Our consciences bear our guilt of sin until cleansed by the forgiving, cleansing grace of God in process of spiritual cleansing, in Christian sanctification.

Regardless of our varying beliefs in the Christian faith and our positions in theology, we are at this point interested in Karl Barth's statement that justification and sanctification are two moments in one action of God. We are interested also with his assertion that while justification is first in order of origin and presupposition, sanctification is first in results.[6] As a recent lecturer has put it, "The tendency in modern Christianity has been to treat the initial stage of God's saving work as the all-important stage, and sanctification as an extra. The sinner must be born again before he can grow up as a child of God, but he is born to grow. The believer is justified to be sanctified; he is adopted as God's child that he may grow into the full stature of the manhood of Christ."[7] God has provided in the Pedilavium the most excellent means for the Christian in this present life to experience and express the forgiveness and cleansing of God. Whenever we practice the triune Holy Communion we proclaim the work of the Triune God: "The Father who hath made me and all the world, the Son, who hath redeemed me and all mankind, and the Holy Spirit who sanctifieth me and all the people of God."[8]

[5] Cf. Muedeking, George, *Emotional Problems and the Bible,* (Philadelphia: Muhlenberg Press, 1956).

[6] Cf. Barth, Karl, *Church Dogmatics,* trans. by G. W. Bromiley, (Edinburgh: T & T Clark, 1958), IV, 2.

[7] Greeves, Frederic, *Theology and the Cure of Souls,* (New York: Channel Press, Inc., 1960), p. 71.

[8] Lowery, C. W., *The Trinity and Christian Devotion,* (New York: Harper and Brother, 1946), p. 77.

Calvin interprets "He that is washed needeth not save to wash his feet," as "renewal." "Again, the other comparison was also applied to the case in hand, that Peter might not set aside the washing of the feet as foolish, for, as Christ washes from the head to the feet those whom he receives as his disciples, so, in those whom he has cleansed, the lower part remains to be daily cleansed. The children of God are not altogether regenerated on the first day, so as to aim at nothing but the heavenly life; but on the contrary, the remains of the flesh continue to dwell in them, with which they maintain a continued struggle throughout their whole life. The term feet, therefore, is metaphorically applied to all passions and cares by which we are brought into contact with the world; for, if the Holy Spirit occupies every part of us, we would no longer have anything to do with the pollutions of the world; but now, by that part in which we are carnal, we creep on the ground, or at least fix our feet in the clay, and, therefore, are to some extent unclean. Thus Christ always finds in us something to cleanse."[9] In this clear commentary Calvin proclaims the soul of the symbol of feet-washing even though he fails to relate it to the logical and natural place, the Pedilavium. The Pedilavium is the most adequate and accurate symbol of the cleansing process that goes on in the life of the believer after baptism.

The early Church Father, Tertullian, describes the sanctifying cleansing of Christ in the symbol of waters: "He Himself invisibly cleanses and that He does to the whole Church without exception. Christ sanctifies. Christ also Himself washed, Himself purifies with the self-same washing of Water by the word, wherein the ministers are seen to do their work in the body."[10] He also writes, "material things raise us to a

[9] Calvin, John, *Commentary on the Gospel According to John,* trans. by W. Pringle, (Grand Rapids: Eerdmans, 1949), p. 59.

[10] Tertullian, "Answer to Pertillian," 111, 49.

recognition of spiritual."[11] To men through the Christian centuries, water as a symbol in the sacraments has meant the forgiving, cleansing grace of Christ through the power of the Holy Spirit. When this sanctifying process restores the fractured relationship between man and God caused by sin, then the communion between man and God becomes "Holy Communion."

The author Luth proclaims the same truth in the following manner: "We may have received forgiveness for our sins once and for all; nevertheless, we frequently need to be forgiven anew because we go on sinning day after day. We may have entered into the love of Jesus Christ, nevertheless we need His love for us to be renewed again and again. That is why Jesus has added the sacrament of Holy Communion to that of Holy Baptism. It is regularly celebrated by the community because our need for it is ever present. At the Holy Communion we are reminded of that unique purification achieved for us on the Cross for all time, and which we cannot and do not have to achieve for ourselves. At the same time, however, we bring to the Lord's table the sins that we are always committing, so that He may do for us what He did for the disciples when He washed their feet. So when we regularly give each other the Holy Communion, we are doing exactly what Jesus bids us do when He says, "For I have given you an example, that ye should do as I have done to you" (John 13:15). The Pedilavium of Holy Communion is the example Christ gave us at the Last Supper in the upper room, and to which He has attached the promise, "If ye know these things, happy are ye if ye do them."

Daily living presses upon us to such an extent that very often God is no longer our Father but a mere religious object. The prevailing atmosphere of the world infects us more than we recognize. If this natural disposition prevails we may be guilty of approaching the intimate sacrament of Com-

[11] Tertullian, "De Baptismo," 5.

munion profanely. The Pedilavium is provided to prepare the body, mind and soul of the earth-bound Christian for Holy Communion. In the symbols of the Christian faith water cleanses, as the bread and the cup feeds. The Christian cannot achieve spiritual action in himself. His part, as a communer, consists in the preparation, opening up a pathway for His grace.

Christ Took A Towel

The practice of the Pedilavium springs not simply from the ground of the common need of earth-bound men, but supremely from the historic narrative. Christians believe that in the life of Christ God approached mankind in a unique manner. The Gospel of John rings throughout with this signal truth, "The word became flesh." Chapter thirteen of John's Gospel likewise begins with this a priori, "knowing that he came from God, and was going unto God." It was the incarnate God who sat as the Head and Host of the Last Supper, who "laid aside his garments, and taking a towel, tied it around him." Let us proceed to examine the historic narrative which is the foundation of Pedilavium in Holy Communion.

"During Supper" is well attested in New Testament manuscripts, and undoubtedly means the Last Supper. There is no indication in the Gospel at what point the act of feet-washing occurred. However, washing after each main course was common, at either Passover meals or fellowship meals. At any one of these points, it would have been very natural for Jesus to institute the Pedilavium, taking the common to symbolize the sacred. This would be in harmony with the Agape and the Eucharist, where Christ also took the common to symbolize the sacred and holy. The fact that the Lord washed the disciples' feet "during Supper" excludes any interpretation that this was an Oriental custom engaged in at the entrance of a dwelling. The washing was at the Supper, rather than at the door, and was given sacramental meaning by the Lord. It was "during Supper" that Christ instituted the component parts of Holy Communion: the Pedilavium, the Agape, and the Eucharist.

The divine nature of Christ includes not only complete knowledge of Himself, but also full knowledge of the hearts of the disciples surrounding His table. The diabolical heart of Judas was as evident to Him as the loving heart of John. In this last night Christ proceeds in full realization that He is the Messiah in the ordained will of God rather than a martyr in the hands of political foes. Judas, in his refusal to have faith in the way of the Lord, becomes a tool of the Devil. The presence of Judas does not signify a falseness or ignorance of Christ; in fact it demonstrates Him as the divine Son of God. The betrayal of the Messiah by a disciple was evident in Old Testament prophecy (Ps. 41:9). Christ selected him with the full knowledge that he would spurn His love and commune with the Devil rather than with His Father (cf. John 13:11; 6:64, 70, 71; 17:12). And before the betrayal Christ declares the occurrence to the other disciples (John 13:19; cf. Isa. 41:26). Thus the presence of Judas corroborates and establishes Jesus as the Christ, the Son of God.

The act of feet-washing begins with the Lord "rising from the supper," laying aside His garments, taking a towel, and girding Himself. The Lord changes His position from Master to servant to enact this part of the Lord's Supper. He lays aside His garment, as He laid aside His glory in the incarnation, as He layeth down His life on the Cross. By His sovereign will and action the work of redemption is initiated and completed. The Lord's laying aside His garments for cleansing is a foreshadowing of the laying down of His life on the Cross for the redemption of sins.

The girding with a towel marks the action of a servant, the "Suffering Servant." The Lord having thus assumed the posture of a servant, undertakes the actions of a servant, "He poureth water into the basin, and began to wash the disciples' feet. . ." The particularity of the description denotes an eye-witness, John. Each step is noted: He rises from among the group; He lays aside the outer garment; He takes a towel and girds Himself; He pours the water into the basin, He washes and wipes the disciples' feet. *When the Messiah served, He served perfectly and completely*.

The towel, basin and water were as much a part of the preparation for the Lord's Supper as the bread and cup. When Jesus instructed the disciples to make ready the Passover, He included all items necessary for the institution of Holy Communion (cf. Matt. 26:19). Because Christ used common items as means for Holy Communion, the disciples' attention was not excited in the preparation. God used the most common means for the glorious manifestation of Himself, even an ignoble birth of an infant child in a stable of the small town of Bethlehem!

"He began to wash and wipe. . ." The disciples looked on as the Lord proceeded, mystified by His action. If the service was the mere Oriental custom which had been forgotten, one of the disciples would undoubtedly have offered to perform the deed. Yet no one offered to take the towel. They did not offer to wash feet any more than they offered to break bread or give the cup, because they could not offer to institute that sacred service which belonged to the exclusive power of Christ.

Scripture does not indicate who was first or last in the service of feet-washing. But "Then He came to Simon Peter," and impulsive Peter was the one to question this new and strange action of Christ. The weakness of Peter was not that he questioned Jesus' action, but that he lacked obedience to Christ. Jesus then gently informed Peter that his questions rested on ignorance. What is Peter's ignorance? Certainly not customary washing of feet. If the washing of feet was a mere lesson to settle the disciples' contention as many interpretations suppose, Peter would not have asked the question; he would have repented and changed places with the Lord. Because Christ was instituting Holy Communion, the meaning of the act could not be understood until the Lord was glorified. The interpretation depended on a full perspective of His Person and His work. The term "shall know" is knowledge (*gnosa*) by experience. After the crucifixion, resurrection, ascension and Pentecost, "after these things," Peter would come to an understanding of what Christ was doing then. Even Christ's commentary on His own action in verses twelve through seventeen is not fully discernible to the disciples until after the complete Christ event. Many teachings and events in Christ's life needed to be interpreted after the crucifixion and the resurrection (cf. John 7:39; 14:26; 16:13). Only by the Spirit can men understand Jesus at all; and His disciples, no less than anyone else, were included here. The real meaning of the Eucharist and the Pedilavium came to the disciples after the complete saving mission of Christ.

Peter presses his disobedience, "By no means shalt thou wash my feet 'for the ages.' " In all eternity (*eis ton aiona*) Peter is to go unwashed by Jesus. Christ meets the extreme disobedience of Peter with the final declaration, "If I do not wash you, 'you are not in fellowship with me' " (John 13:8). Peter suggests eternal disobedience; therefore Christ's condition is eternal. The immediate verses speak of the washing of Peter's feet, and the whole passage deals with feet-washing; therefore the washing that is prerequisite to having a share in the Kingdom of God is logically the washing of sins in the blood of Christ that is symbolized in the Christian service of baptism and the Pedilavium. The present, "thou hast," (*echeis*) is not futuristic, but timeless. It connotes eternity and universality, "Unless Jesus washes a person, that person has no part!"

Peter makes a complete change: "Not my feet only, but wash my hands and head as well" (John 13:9). Christ then proceeds to distinguish between the sacraments of Christian baptism and the Pedilavium of Holy Communion. "A man who has bathed needs no further washing except to wash his feet" (John 13:10). The "washing" of the feet is contrasted with the "bathing" of the whole body. The text uses two distinct words, *leloumenos* for bathing, and *nipsosthai* for washing. The "washing" does not connote essential change, but is related to the change already wrought. The two "cleansings" are related but distinct. In Christian baptism man as man is made clean. However, Christian man is still human and is prone to sinning as long as he lives "in the flesh." This same interpretation of the passage is given by C. H. Dodd: "In John 13:10 to take a bath is contrasted with to wash a part of the body. Baptism is a bath *(loutron,* Eph. 5:26, Tit. 3:5). The Christian reader is assured that having undergone the bath he is clean yet may need some kind of recurrent washing."[12] The paradox of the continuous cleansing from sin after Christian baptism is expressed in First John: "If we claim to be sinless, we are self-deceived and strangers to the truth. If we confess our sins, he is just, and may be trusted to forgive our sins, and to cleanse us from every kind of wrong. . . My children, in writing this to you my purpose is that you should not commit sin, but should one commit a sin, we have one to plead our cause with the Father, Jesus Christ, and he is just" (I John 1:8; 2:1). Lenski writes in his commentary, "As the body is clean altogether when it is washed in the dusty road, so we are spiritually clean when Jesus has washed away our sin and guilt; we need only a minor cleansing when we move about in this sinful world with its impure contacts."[13] The words of Christ, "If I wash thee not, thou hast no part with me" make it impossible to remove the idea of cleansing from sin in the Pedilavium from Holy Communion.

[12] Dodd, C. H., *The Interpretation of the Fourth Gospel,* (Cambridge: University Press, 1955), p. 401.

[13] Lenski, R. C. H., *St. John's Gospel,* (Columbus: Lutheran Book Concern, 1942), p. 921.

The disciples are clean through their submission to an action of Jesus which relies for its efficacy upon its relation to Him, to His crucifixion and resurrection. It is primarily an act of God to man. God alone has the power to cleanse the heart and soul of man from sin. Man's administration of and participation in the sacramental symbols require the surrendering of self-will and position. Attaining humility is never the purpose of a service like feet-washing. Humility is a spiritual attribute wrought by the Holy Spirit in man when he surrenders completely to God. Humility cannot be the objective of the Lord's washing the disciples' feet, for this would be self-humility, like self-righteousness, which is vain and worthless. The Gospel of Christ does not conquer and cleanse the world of sin by our humble service, but by the grace of Christ through the Cross which was His victory over sin and death.

The truth of the partial defilement of the person has a parallel in the truth of the partial defilement of society, "and ye are clean, but not all." The disciples as a whole were clean, even though there was one in the midst who refused to be cleansed by Christ. The presence of Judas did not change the general character of the Lord's disciples any more than the contacting of sin by the Christian eliminates his new life in Christ. Neither does the presence of some unregenerate persons in the church destroy it as the body of Christ. The process of cleansing and purging is continuous in every beliver and every group of believers until the end of time.

In verses twelve through seventeen Christ gives an interpretation of His washing the disciples' feet. The disciples' full understanding of this commentary is contingent upon the coming of the spirit of truth. The full significance of the action can be understood only after His Cross and resurrection, when the Gospel is complete. However, Jesus does give a complete commentary on His action and then commands its institution as a part of the triune Holy Communion. Christ clearly explains His intention in washing the feet of the disciples. The Pedilavium had a spiritual significance related to and integrated with the institution of Holy Communion. The Last Supper in the upper room was the merging of the old and the new, and the Gospel of John has recorded the relationship of the two feasts, the old and the new, the Passover and the Holy Communion. In the Old Covenant the priests who served in the service of Communion with the Almighty were commanded to cleanse themselves symbolically by washing their hands and feet at the laver which stood before the door of the tabernacle (Exod. 30:19-21). In the New Covenant we are commanded to cleanse ourselves symbolically from defilement by sin before partaking of the sacred elements of the Eucharist. It is this preparation and cleansing that make us fit to enter into "Holy" Communion with the living God. To the Corinthians Paul writes that unworthy participation in Holy Communion will bring spiritual death. The Pedilavium is the New Testament antitype of the Old Testament type in the laver. Christians as New Covenant priests are required to cleanse themselves before daring to participate in the most sacred service of the Christian faith, the Eucharist.

"Know ye" means "Do you apprehend, perceive, understand the meaning of feet-washing?" This type of knowledge is apprehended through experience, in contrast to knowledge that is attained by intellectual pursuit. Christ posed the deeper inquiry, "Do you really understand?" Jesus intended that the full import of what they had seen Him do to them be brought to their realization. Christ was not concerned in humbling them by washing their feet, but in making them like Himself in the New Order. The question here, "know ye?" has the same import as the question that is often asked, "Do you know Christ as your Savior?" Christ was not seeking erudition in the disciples, but spiritual experiences as He does in the lives of all disciples, even those "who have not seen and yet believe."

When He says, "You call me The Teacher and The Lord," "you" is emphatic, meaning, you who have been with me as my disciples, you who call me "The Teacher and the Lord." Out of all my followers do "you" apprehend my action? Both titles, "Teacher and Lord," have the article "The." Of all men to whom the title has been accorded, He was "The Teacher." With the additional title "Lord," Christ was more than an eminent human teacher. We dare not take the title "Teacher" by itself and rationalize Him to be one of a class of men. These titles as used by Christ designate His divine-human nature, God-man, "God in Christ."

Upon the basis of Jesus being the Christ, the Son of God, we are indebted to obey His word and example. As explained before, the term "ought" is more accurately translated "owe." It is the same word used in First John, "It is by this that we know what love is: that Christ laid down his life for us. And we in our turn are bound to lay down our lives for our brothers" (I John 3:16). The ordinary term "ought" implies "tit for tat," which is a wrong motive for any Christian action of service. The real meaning of "ought" is related to the fact, "You do not belong to yourselves; you were bought at a price," and, "Offer your very selves to Him a living sacrifice" (I Cor. 6:20; Rom. 12:1). Christ presented His commentary from the greater to the lesser. The basis of the sacramental symbol and command is Christ Himself.

"For I have given you an example" deserves our careful attention. Nowhere else does Christ tell us that He has given us an example. We are not at liberty to take His life, without reserve, as a subject of imitation. We cannot take His life without reserve as an example, for He was uniquely the only divinely begotten Son of God, on a divine mission. The Gospel is concluded: "It is finished," and unrepeatable. Thus the theologians who interpret His whole life and teaching as a supreme example, and the people who try to practice the Christian faith as mere followers of an "Example" are not imitators, but apes. Christ was not different from us in degree, but in kind. "Example theology and practice" are humanism of the worst kind. Therefore, when Christ commands that we follow His example, His command is distinct and has special meaning. We cannot follow His atoning sacrifice for sins on the Cross, but we can enter into His life through the sacramental symbols of Holy Communion.

Three different words are translated "example" in the New Testament. That which is translated "example" here is *hupodeigma.* The same word is used in other passages (cf. Heb. 4:11, 8:5; 9:23; Jas. 5:10; II Pet. 2:6), sometimes translated "examples" and sometimes "patterns." For instance, "See, saith he, that you make everything according to the pattern (example) shown you on the mount" (Heb. 8:5). In another passage it is translated "copies," "It was necessary therefore that the copies (examples) of the things in the heavens should be cleansed with these . . ." (Heb. 9:23). The Brethren missionary and author, C. F. Yoder, gives this comment, "These 'copies,' therefore, pointed forward to something better, just as the 'copy' or 'pattern' or 'symbol' or 'example' which Jesus gave in feet-washing points to the spiritual cleansing of the heart and the holiness of the kingdom to come. . . Let no man then say that it was only an example in hospitality, or an object lesson. The very sentence in which the word is found shows that it means more than an example of character. Jesus did not say, 'I have given you an example that you should be as I have been' (humble), but he did say, 'do as I have done.' "[14]

Christ, anticipating the reaction of His disciples toward His command to wash feet, emphasizes His serious intent by the words, "Truly, truly, I say to you, a servant is not greater than his lord; nor one sent than the one that sent him." Christ here exhorts all disciples to evaluate their true position by the comparison of slave to master, of man to God. This added emphasis on the menial service of the Pedilavium seemed necessary because of the basic sin of pride and vanity in the heart of man. The recurrent pride of man needs continual abase-

[14] Yoder, C. F., *God's Means of Grace,* (Elgin, Illinois: Brethren Publishing House, 1908), pp. 298-312.

ment. The Jews turned away from Jesus as the Messiah because their religious pride prevented them from seeing the real majesty in His menial ministry. If we as Christians consider ourselves too "modern" to stoop to wash feet in Holy Communion, we need to consider the stooping of Christ from the heavenly glory to the Cross. Christ drew a comparison between Himself and His followers that eliminated any objection to this menial service. The twelve are not only to be disciples, but the Lord's own apostles, (*apostolos*); and yet even this high position does not elevate them above the service of the Pedilavium. However, is it not true that the Church today tends to avoid a sort of Master who washes people's feet? Is it not true that the Church seeks to rule rather than to serve? If the Church tries to rule in the earthly sense, instead of being a servant of the Lord, it comes under the shadow of Judas.

Holy blessedness does not depend upon knowing the truth, but upon doing the truth. "If you know these things, blessed are you if you keep doing them." A sacrament is constituted by a command and a promise. In the Pedilavium we have both, "Do as I have done," and "happy are ye if ye do them." In the shadow of sadness Christ spoke of happiness. At the time when everything pointed to death, Christ directed them to the way of a happy life. Knowledge alone does not bring happiness. Throughout the time of the upper room Christ emphasized action upon the basis of knowledge. Doing is emphatic over against mere knowing. The word for blessed (*makarios*) is the same one used in the beatitudes. It is significant because it denotes the joy and the satisfaction arising from knowing and experiencing the divine blessings of God. The promise of the happiness is made only "if you keep doing them." The very nature of the entire Christian faith and Christian sacraments is to keep expressing and experiencing itself.

Walter Lüthi speaks of the need of spiritual happiness in the Christian world. "A conversation I had with an experienced lay-preacher the other day surprised me to a certain extent, and gave me much food for thought. He was relating his experiences to me, and told me that when he meets people to whom life has been cruel, and who are so embittered and crushed that they are no longer capable of love, he usually advises them to go often to Holy Communion all the same. He tells them that in this way the battered garden of their lives will be replanted. Because of the war, so much crushed and hardened ground is being restored to usefulness in our drive of increased cultivation. Yet there is crushed and hardened ground not only in our parks and outside our houses, but also inside, in marriages and families up and down the country. There are so many gardens of life in which no flower blooms any more, and no bird sings, and in which the fruit of charity will never ripen again. Come and let these barren gardens be replanted, for Christ wants flowers to bloom and birds to sing in them and the fruits of brotherly love to thrive."[15] "If you know these things, blessed are you if you keep doing them."

Symbolism in John's Gospel

Water symbolism in John thirteen is a familiar concept in the Gospel. In fact the characteristic style of John's distinctive Gospel is symbolism. It alone contains the three great passages of the sheep-fold, the Good Shepherd, and the Vine, which have always been a basis for Christian art and architecture. There are not only these specific symbolic teachings, but also the general spirit of symbolism which forms their style. The writer describes the select incidents from the life of the incarnate Christ by the term "signs" (*sameia*). The modern concept of incident cannot define the select events in the Lord's ministry used by John. They are "signs" because they direct men to look beneath the surface of the event for the revelation of the deeper work and will of God. Each sign had a double quality, the visible and the invisible. The visible

[15] Lüthi, Walter, *St. John's Gospel*, (Virginia: Richmond, John Knox Press, 1960), p. 181.

aspect of the event was referred to by John as a "work," in that it was manifested in and related to the phenomenon of life. The invisible aspect of the event was the revelation of the divine truth beneath the surface perceived in the context of faith. Insofar as the invisible truth was perceived in the visible works, John calls them "signs." They are signs because they reveal the mysteries which underlie the visible world of events. Thus, the importance of the sign depended on what it indicated, rather than on what it was. Whenever the term "sign" is used in the Gospel of John, it is always with the distinct reference to the invisible character which the work or miracle indicated. Those who termed them "signs" attached to Christ divine attributes in faith, and each sign gave occasion to a growth of belief or unbelief according to the will of those who witnessed it.[16]

All the material included in this select Gospel story is relevant to the object of belief and confession of faith in Christ. There is an unmistakable harmony within the different parts of the fourth Gospel; thus, each part must be considered not only in itself, but also in relation to the others with which it is connected. John's Gospel is characterized by faith that is interpreted by thought, and thought by fact: that the historical unity of the book is interwoven by a spiritual unity. The broad plan of the Gospel is: (1) the ministry of the incarnate Christ (1:19-21:50), and (2) the meaning of the ministry of the incarnate Christ (13-21). By this outline of the Gospel the thirteenth chapter is the prelude to the second main section. It is in the section and related to the institution of the sacraments in the upper room (John 13; cf. Matt. 26:26-29; Mark 14:22-25; Luke 22:19-20), the last discourses on the Holy Spirit and spiritual life (John 13:31; 16), the priestly prayer of our Lord (John 17), the passion of our Lord (John 18, 19), and the resurrection of the triumphant

[16] Cf. Westcott, B. F., *The Gospel According to St. John,* (London: Murray, 1908), p. 189.

Christ (John 20, 21). Because of the definite plan of the Gospel, the thirteenth chapter must be interpreted by these selected signs in the second section of which they are a part. The setting of the narrative of feet-washing is not physical cleansing but spiritual cleansing, not service but sacrifice, not creaturely humility but Holy Communion.

In view of the importance of symbolism in John's Gospel the narrative of feet-washing in the thirteenth chapter has spiritual significance. The double quality of the signs points at once not to the visible act, but to the higher understanding in the context of faith. The cleansing of the disciples' feet represents their cleansing from sin by Christ. "When the necessity of this cleansing is told to Peter, he asks that not only his feet but also his head and hands be washed. Just as the Cross is the temporal manifestation of the eternal movement of Christ from the Father who sends Him into the world, and again from the world to the Father, so the feet-washing is enacted by Jesus in full recognition of the same fact."[17]

In relation to our subject it is striking to note that throughout the Gospel of John there is an extraordinary attention given to water as a sign, or symbol, and that it is used as the visible means for the invisible power of God. In chapter one there is the account of John the Baptist and the baptism of Jesus. In chapter two Christ attends the marriage at Cana, where the water is changed into wine. In chapter three Nicodemus comes to Jesus by night inquiring about this new life, and Jesus tells him that he must be born of water and spirit. In chapter four Jesus meets the woman at the well and talks about living water. In chapter five Jesus heals a paralyzed man at the pool by the sheep-gate. In chapter nine there is recorded the healing of the man born blind, waiting at the pool of Siloam. And in chapter thirteen there is the washing of the disciples' feet. It is not the intention of this study to

[17] Barrett, C. K. *The Gospel According to St. John,* (London: S.P.C.K., 1955), p. 363.

force a scheme upon all these events which give attention to water as a "sign." However, it would be equally wrong to ignore them and their significant relation to the Pedilavium. Certainly, it is evident that John's Gospel uses water as a sign for the cleansing, healing power of God.

In John's Gospel the symbol of water comes as early as the prologue. Both in the baptizing of John and in the baptism of Jesus, the spiritual meaning of the physical event is evidenced. The Baptist insisted that his baptizing was not an end in itself. He explained to the Jewish committee, "He who sent me to baptize in water has told me, 'When you see the Spirit coming down upon someone and resting upon him, you will know that this is he who is to baptize in the Holy Spirit'" (John 1:33), contrasting the symbol of water with the Holy Spirit. The baptizing of John was a mere sign, a symbol, of the Messiah to come, indeed, who was present. We see in the narrative of Jesus' baptism the essence of the spiritual in the physical. Jesus demanded the physical baptism by the hands of John as a sign of His entering His ministry, and in a sense to institute Christian baptism. That He was called "The Lamb of God" immediately sets forth that Christian baptism is connected with death. "Thus there stands right at the beginning of John's Gospel the reference to the institution of Christian baptism by Him who, as the Lamb, has removed the sin of the world and has therefore fulfilled the meaning of all baptism and brought baptism with the Spirit."[18]

The water signs in the Gospel of John, taken one at a time, would not lend much weight to the interpretation of the feet-washing as a sacramental symbol. However, when they are studied together in the symbolism of the Gospel they bring a sacramental meaning to feet-washing that is irrevocable. The Pedilavium is certainly not a "coincidence" in the fourth Gospel, but a part of a grand design of symbolism to

[18] Cullmann, Oscar, *Early Christian Worship,* trans. J. B. Torrance and A. S. Todd, (London: SCM Press, 1959), p. 65.

show man, who is slow to perceive the spiritual, the cleansing, forgiving, renewing power of the Holy Spirit through the symbol of water. When the narratives are studied carefully there is the recognition of detail and the personal touch of one who witnessed the events, one who beheld them as signs of the revelation of God in Christ. The symbolism of water in the Gospel of John places the feet-washing in a theological context. The Lord's washing of the disciples' feet during the Last Supper places it in a sacramental setting.

The Cosmic Circle of Christ

The weight of the significance of John thirteen is in the cosmic circle of Christ. Christ "came forth from God," fulfilled His mission in the flesh, and "returned to God." The phrase, "He did come out from God" declares His deity, His oneness with God, and His incarnate invasion into the world. The phrase, "he went to God" declares His ascension back to this very God. The divine movement is always cirular, beginning and concluding with God. Humanism is the converse from this movement where man presumes to think that everything begins and ends in himself. However, the divine circle, within it man and the whole cosmos, is expressed by Moses in the symbol of "The everlasting arms" (Deut. 33:27). In the prelude to the passage John summarizes this significance in four phrases: (1) "that he should depart out of this world unto the Father," (2) "that the Father had given all things into His hands," (3) "that He came forth from God," (4) "and was going to God." The incarnate Christ is returning to the eternal glory with the Father who placed in His hands the whole efficacy of salvation.

It was God in Christ who sat with His family of brethren in the upper room. Thus every incident of the supper room must be interpreted by the fact that it was the word and deed of God. The ponderous fact that here was God who washed feet, who ate, who talked at a supper is overwhelming. To the nonbeliever, to sophisticated society, to the wilful world, these mundane acts of Christ are nonsense. To the believer this is the sublime truth, that God has condescended to sinful man to cleanse his sins. The divine truth of Christianity is that the highest must become the lowest – or it would not be the highest.

It was the very Son of God, with full divine authority, who spoke and acted. The fixed framework of this New Testament passage is that it was God in Christ who spoke and commanded, who initiated and concluded, who promised and fulfilled. "The Master and the Lord" of the upper room who girded Himself with a towel and washed the disciples' feet was God's special envoy. He was the One who revealed the nature of the invisible God. Our belief in the credence of God in Christ determines our belief in the credence of John thirteen as a sacramental doctrine. As in the Gospel of Matthew, "Full authority in heaven and on earth has been committed to me" (Matt. 28:18), so here in the Gospel of John "all things" is without limitation of any kind. "To Him" means that the purpose of God is in Christ to do as He wills. In view of these divine truths concerning the Son of God the passage has a divine dimension.

When the narrative of feet-washing is not accepted as an obvious sacramental doctrine, then there arise many perplexing problems of interpretation. A New Testament scholar who does not accept the narrative as a sacramental doctrine writes, "This is one of the most difficult passages to interpret in the whole New Testament. It is unique – there is nothing comparable to it in the other gospels."[19] Another Christian theologian describes the passage with its implications as "obscure."[20] The suggestion that the feet-washing represents the Eucharist, that it "symbolizes all that is implied in the

[19] Grant, Frederick G., *The Gospel of John,* (New York: Harper and Brothers, 1956), Vol. II, p. 7.
[20] Barrett, *op. cit.,* p. 368.

Eucharist,"[21] is theological evasion which is totally unacceptable. For qualified New Testament scholars to speak of the narrative of feet-washing as "the most difficult passage," or "obscure" betrays the fact that they refuse the obvious interpretation and lack a suitable substitute. Likewise, the interpretation which suggests that feet-washing represents the Eucharist is confusing. The Eucharist symbolizes the broken body and shed blood of Christ and cannot, in turn, be represented by the feet-washing. The Lord designated the distinctive symbolic meaning of each part of Holy Communion: the Pedilavium symbolizes cleansing; the Agape symbolizes the community of God; and Eucharist symbolizes Calvary. Each symbol is distinct and cannot be represented by a secondary symbol. If for no other reason, these very inadequate interpretations force a serious New Testament student to accept the narrative of feet-washing as a sacramental doctrine. However, the compelling reason for Christians to believe in the feet-washing as a sacramental doctrine is that during the passion of the Lord He deliberately set forth a pattern to copy with a promise of happiness to all who fulfill it.

Some relate the Lord's washing of the disciples' feet to the strife that is recorded in Luke 22:24-30, as His answer to the general argument among the disciples about position and precedence in the material kingdom which Christ was to establish. Each was urging his own claim, and angering the others by his own pretensions. The argument then proposes that at the time of the Last Supper the disciples are so angry with one another that they refuse to wash the dust from each other's feet, and the feet of the Master. To quote an interpreter, "One supposes that, as a rule, on arriving at their destination, it was their practice to take turns at washing off the dust of the roads from the sandaled feet of the little brotherhood, and that they

[21] MacGregor, G. H. C., *Eucharistic Origins,* (London: Clarke, 1928), p. 226.

did it willingly, as a matter of course, and thought nothing about it. But tonight all of them sat stubbornly in their places and would have none of the menial duty."[22] Thus the Lord seized the opportunity and acted out a parable of humility.

One recognizes immediately that this interpretation of John thirteen is based upon supposition. The above quoted interpretation begins, "One supposes." To interpret the longest recorded narrative of the Lord's words and actions during the last night in the upper room by "supposition" appears in serious error. The error becomes all the more evident when it is compared with the other narratives of the upper room, the eucharistic sayings, which are interpreted literally in great detail by most church doctrines of Communion. In other words, the doctrine of the "bread and cup," the Eucharist, is founded upon a few verses in the Synoptic Gospels, and rightly so. But at the same time a consistent consideration of the New Testament Scriptures must include the comparatively lengthy complete narrative in John thirteen of feet-washing in Holy Communion. The complete Holy Communion service, as instituted by our Lord in the upper room, must include all that God in Christ said and did. To give lengthy consideration to the bread and cup, to the exclusion of the Agape and the Pedilavium, is not "rightly dividing the word of truth." The service of triune Holy Communion was instituted by our Lord in His passion at the Last Supper and recorded in New Testament Scriptures.

Another misinterpretation of the narrative of feet-washing is that it was just an Oriental custom, not the institution of a Christian sacrament for the practice of the Church. This interpretation does not take into account the fact that it was the custom for each person to wash his own feet, rather than the duty of the master of the house (cf. Gen. 18:14; 19:2; Judg. 19:21). It also loses sight of the fact that the Lord's

[22] Gossip, Arthur John, *Interpreter's Bible,* (New York: Abingdon-Cokesbury Press, 1952), Vol. VIII, p. 680.

washing of the disciples' feet took place during supper, rather than at the door before the supper began. The strongest argument against this interpretation is that "The account says not a word, gives not a hint, of this being a washing for physical cleansing; but all the way through it is given a spiritual significance."[23] Jesus related it with baptism and salvation, not a mere custom. Also the full meaning could be had by the disciples only after the death and resurrection of Christ, the basis of the interpretation of its meaning.

A commonly-held misinterpretation of the narrative of feet-washing is that it was a parable in humility. Of course the Lord demonstrated humility in washing the disciples' feet, as He did in every act of His earthy ministry. However, this cannot be the basic interpretation because, for one thing, humility is the result of the spirit of humbleness, not the act of washing feet. A person cannot "do humility," he can only be humble through the spirit of Christ. This argument is a mere supposition based on the unfounded theory that Christ washed the disciples' feet to settle their quarrel. The Scriptures themselves prohibit such a supposition and interpretation. The Lord defined it as a symbol of cleansing: "If I wash thee not, thou has no part with me." According to the Scriptures the feet-washing took place during the Agape, before the Eucharist, thus before the contention as recorded in Luke. This interpretation of the narrative of feet-washing as an acted parable of humility is not in accordance with the New Testament Scriptures. It seems rather obvious that in the midst of His passion in the upper room the Lord is not concerned with an acted parable of humility, but with the institution of the sacrament of Holy Communion.

The feet-washing in John's Gospel begins the narration of the passion of the incarnate God. The eternal hour of the Cross has come. Thus the washing of the disciples' feet is related to the death and resurrection of our Lord. The

[23] Yoder, *op. cit.*, pp. 298-312.

Pedilavium is certainly not an unrelated action containing in itself a mere ethical lesson in humility. This "humility interpretation" is foreign not only to the context of the passage, but also to the Gospel of John. The entire Gospel of John, which seeks an active saving faith in the Lord Jesus Christ, the Son of God, and the particular passage of pathos and passion speak against such a feeble interpretation. To interpret the feet-washing as a mere lesson in ethics is to ignore its strategic place in the passion of Christ, preceding the institution of the sacrament of the Eucharist. The Greek scholar, Westcott, writes, "The central idea of this record corresponds with one aspect of the institution of the Eucharist, that of self-sacrifice. The incident evidently belongs to the same spiritual circumstances" as the Eucharist of Holy Communion.[24]

The first main division in John's Gospel is a collection of select narratives of Christ's earthly ministry (John 1:18-12:50); the second main division is the meaning of this ministry. Chapter thirteen begins the second main division of John's Gospel, the passion of Christ. The whole purpose of His incarnation is to save whosoever will accept His salvation. That was the purpose of His coming, the end of His earthly ministry, and the dream of His heart. John chapter thirteen begins this presentation of the saving passion of Christ. The Gospel of John alone gives us a report of the Pedilavium, the last words of Christ, and the last prayer with His disciples at the time of the institution of Holy Communion. This most sacred legacy which the Lord has left us can never be interpreted accurately or fully, except by the heart which enters into the secret place of the Most High. The infinite disclosure of divine love and grace is only to the one who enters into Communion in the spirit of Christ.

The prelude to the thirteenth chapter of John's Gospel strikes the note of the whole presentation of the passion and gives us the key for accurate interpretation. "Now before

24 Westcott, *op. cit.*, p. 189.

the Passover festival, Jesus, knew that his hour had come and he must leave this world and go to the Father. He had always loved his own who were in this world, and now he was to show the full extent of his love" (John 13:1). The "feast of Passover" in verse one and the "supper" in verse two refer to the same Supper that is described in Matthew 26:26-29, Mark 14:22-25, and Luke 22:19-20.

Peter requests that the Lord wash not only his feet, but his whole body to be "doubly sure" of his cleansing from sin. Jesus refuses his request with the statement that he who is completely bathed, *leloumenos*, needs only to have his feet washed. As the New Testament scholar, Cullmann, writes, "These words can surely have only this meaning: he who has received Baptism, even when he sins afresh, needs no second Baptism, for one cannot be twice baptized. The reference of the word 'bathed' to Baptism is the more convincing that baptism in early Christianity did actually consist of dipping the whole body in the water. . . According to this story one thing is necessary, that for sins committed after Baptism the disciples should go on celebrating the Eucharist in fellowship with Christ and the brethren. Baptism is once, it cannot be repeated, just as the death of Christ cannot be repeated. There is, however, a sacrament which is to be repeated, which is meant to be repeated, the Sacrament of the fellowship of love, the Lord's Supper. This is the meaning of the words, 'save to wash his feet,' in verse 10."[25] While Cullmann relates the necessity of repetition to Communion in general, we relate it specifically to feet-washing, according to the words of God in Christ, "Ye owe it to one another to wash the feet; for an example I gave you that ye should do as I have done to you."

The same New Testament teacher who suggested that the feet-washing represented the Eucharist writes, "But there is surely significance in the fact that this rite takes the place occupied in the Synoptics by the institution of the Lord's

[25] Cullmann, *op. cit.,* pp. 108-109.

Supper. . . Moreover 'he who has bathed does not need to wash, except for his feet.' " So far as there is any allusion to the sacraments, is it fanciful to see baptism typified by the washing of the whole body, and the Eucharist by the washing of the feet, the rite which for John takes the place of the institution of the Eucharist and carries its values? "For those who are true disciples, the experience of regeneration symbolized in their initial Baptism has no need to be repeated. What does need to be repeated is the 'washing of the feet' – the removal of life's travel-stains by communion with their Lord."[26] Here again the command and necessity of repeating the sacraments is set forth, although incorrectly applied only to the bread and cup, rather than correctly applied to the Agape, the Pedilavium, and the Eucharist. "He that is bathed needeth not. . ." makes a clear distinction between bathing of the whole person and washing of the feet, between baptism and feet-washing. The one who is baptized, and thus cleansed, needs only to wash what has become soiled in his daily walk; so he who by the washing of regeneration of baptism has been once cleansed of his sin (Titus 3:5) needs only to come to Christ hereafter for forgiveness and redemption from those sins which are in some sense the result of daily life. A person need not come again and again for the washing of regeneration of sin in baptism, but only for the cleansing of daily sins. We who have been baptized, bathed, still need to be constantly washed by Christ. The need for constant cleansing has been graciously provided for in the Christian faith and worship by the sacraments of triune Holy Communion.

Christ's commands to repeat the sacrament of the bread and cup and the feet-washing are in a sense parallel. In relation to the eucharistic command Jesus says, "this do in remembrance of me" (Luke 22:19; I Cor. 11:24). In relation to the Pedila-

[26] MacGregor, G. H. C., "The Eucharist in the Fourth Gospel," *New Testament Studies,* (London: Cambridge University Press), Vol. 9, No. 2, pp. 112, 113.

vium Jesus says in three different ways, (1) "ye ought also to wash one another's feet," (2) "I have given you an example that ye should do as I have done to you," and (3) "If ye know these things, happy are ye if ye do them." If we are to interpret literally the commands of Christ, the command of feet-washing as a perpetual observance is even more explicit than that for the bread and cup. The command to repeat the sacrament of the bread and cup is in the form of a simple request; the command to repeat the feet-washing is thrice repeated. The term of command "ought" connotes a simple moral sense of duty. However, the Greek term is more accurately translated as "owing" through the debt incurred by the cost of the Cross. There is the same divine "must" to our faith in fulfilling the will of Christ as there was to His life in fulfilling the will of God the Father.

In the upper room Christ instituted means for disciples of all time to worship and express their saving faith in Him, following His crucifixion, resurrection, and ascension to the Father. The nature of man requires means to worship, and here Christ is providing sacramental symbols to worship Him as the crucified, resurrected Redeemer of the world. This truth is so aptly stated: "We need symbols of recollection and repentance, of devotion and affirmation, of appreciation and apprehension, and of communion and communication. Symbols that will take us up and out of the workaday world into that strange new world of God, and back into the world in the spirit and power of that spiritual experience. 'I kiss my child not only to show my love, but also to love my child more . . .' The drama of feet-washing is grounded in an event in the upper room that has universal relevance to the fulfillment of man's life. For us, it is a symbol, a doorway into life, a kind of altar-stairs upon which the angel of God descends to us and we ascend to God."[27] The eternal God

[27] Weimer, Glen, "Symbols in Religious Practice," *Brethren Life and Thought*. (Elgin, Illinois), Vol. IV, No. 4, pp. 24, 27.

in Christ fulfilled our continuing need of experiencing His cleansing grace in the sacramental symbol of the Pedilavium.

Basic to the Pedilavium is the fact that the events of the upper room come to us by the authority of God. Because God was in Christ, there is the sense of absolute sovereignty in all that was spoken and done in the upper room. Even though there was a traitor, treachery and death, yet there was His power of the resurrection which overcame all evil and death. The same God in Christ who washed the disciples' feet is King of kings and Lord of lords. The first and the thirteenth chapters of John's Gospel have the same Person as the beginning and basis of it all. "In the beginning was the Word, and the Word was with God, and the Word was God," and "Jesus knowing that the Father had given all things into his hands, and that he was come from God, and went to God" are one and the same Person. This is the inescapable approach to the interpretation of the narrative of feet-washing in the thirteenth chapter of John's Gospel. "Christ's presence hallows the commonest events and turns the meanest elements into the richest."[28]

[28] Plummer, A., *St. John,* (Cambridge: University Press, 1890), p. xliv.

4

The Love-Feast

HOLY COMMUNION FROM THE VERY BEGINNING WAS A FELLOWSHIP meal, a fellowship between each believer and God as well as each believer and his brother.[1] The Christian faith creates an inescapable fellowship of *agape* expressed in all of life and supremely in Communion. In the Love-feast of Communion the Church is meeting together in the truest sense as the Body of Christ. Among many members of the Church Communion has come to mean an altar table at the front of the sanctuary which is reverently untouched. This practice in effect reestablishes the separating veil of the Old Covenant which was irrevocably removed at Calvary. Churches are experimenting; peoples of the world are counterfeiting in many practices in order to gain this lost sense of fellowship. Christians of every kind need the fellowship of love in the sacrament of the Love-feast.

The life of our Lord was filled with fellowships. Many

[1] Cf. Phillips, J. B., *Appointment with God,* (London: Wyvern Books, 1954), p. 39.

times in the Gospels Jesus takes His place as head of the household at their meals and banquets. His fellowship with His disciples might be described as a "table-fellowship."[2] Christ began His ministry at a feast (John 2:1-11), and on many occasions used eating fellowships to teach (Matt. 8:15; 9:10; 11:9; 14:13-21; 15:2; 16:6; Mark 3:20; 8:19; 66:14; Luke 5:29; 7:36; 9:10-17, 24:30; John 2:1-11; 6:5-13; 4:27; 12:2). Twice He fed multitudes miraculously (Matt. 16:9, 10), and the scribes and Pharisees complained that He ate and drank with publicans and sinners (Luke 15:2). When He drew near to the last earthly night He gave no instructions concerning the Church, but detailed instructions concerning the Last Supper. He ordained that a Love-feast, connected in a mystical way with His death and resurrection, should be instituted for Holy Communion.

The secret of the early Christian Church in reaching the world with its faith was the "fellowship of love," the *Koinonia of agape*.[3] This fellowship of love transformed a band of Galilean strangers in an upstairs room in Jerusalem into a "body" that in less than twenty years was being described in distant Macedonia as "turning the world upside down" (Acts 17:6). And within three hundred years the Roman Empire acknowledged this fellowship as the religion of the state. The key word in the fellowship was "brother," and the early Christian literature gives clear evidence that it was used with a sense of precious reality. Men became brothers as they became embraced by the *agape* of God into the family of God. The fellowship of love is the essence of the early Church, the framework into which came the tremendous spiritual power which transformed lives and the world.

Ecumenicity in its purest form is the Love-feast of Holy

[2] Keating, J. F., *The Agape and the Christ,* (London: Methuen & Co., 1901), p. 37.

[3] Baillie, John, *The Place of Jesus Christ in Modern Christianity,* (Edinburgh: T. & T. Clark, 1929), p. 41.

Communion. This fellowship to which all believers are called joins the forces of evangelism in the vast scheme of reconciliation and redemption. Each individual believer is brought together with every other believer in the Agape, forming the great force of righteousness in the world. The Love-feast welds a sacred solidarity out of our splintered society. In the Love-feast men of God meet together in the deepest sense provided for us by Christ.

The Love-Feast in the Apostolic Period

The New Testament does not contain many references concerning the early worship practices of the Church. However, it is evident from the references that the Love-feast was a component part of Communion. Probably one main reason for the scarcity of direct references to worship in the New Testament lay in its being so simple in form, and altogether so much the natural and congenial thing that it called for no special comment from those who were steeped in it. No one talks or thinks much about the air he breathes, so long as it is fresh and pure!

We believe that Jesus Christ instituted the Holy Communion as practiced by the Church. Some scholars cast doubt on whether or not this rite was instituted by Christ. However, the Church practiced it immediately following the ascension of the Lord and Pentecost (Acts 2:42, 46). The Gospels record the Last Supper in relation to the passion of the Lord in a way that makes it obviously the rite of their time. We cannot force ourselves to believe that the repetition of the Last Supper just grew up or was adopted from pagan cults. The resurrected Christ of the Christian faith stood in contrast, not affinity, to the surrounding pagan cults. The Gospel writers had direct access to the words of the Lord. Paul received his Gospel from direct revelation, which was later confirmed by the apostles in Jerusalem. Paul visited Jerusalem three years after his conversion (Gal. 1:18), which was just six years after the Last Supper, and Paul taught the practice of Holy Communion, using the sayings of Jesus Christ at the Last Supper. Never in New Testament time was the sacrament of Holy Communion, instituted by Christ, questioned.

The essence of the Love-feast can best be understood in the Apostolic period by our examining the practice of it in Scripture. Although the New Testament does not contain many explicit passages concerning detailed worship, yet it is astonishingly rich in material which demonstrates the warmth and inward depth of fellowship among the Christian brethren. In fact this "fellowship" worship has been singled out as being the most distinctive quality of the new movement. The Scripture passages in Acts relating the practice of Holy Communion in the Apostolic period are as follows:

"They met constantly to hear the apostles teach, and to share the common life, to break bread, and to pray" (Acts 2:42). "With one mind they kept up their daily attendance at the temple, and breaking bread in private houses, shared meals with unaffected joy, as they praised God and enjoyed the favour of the whole people. And day by day added to their number those whom he was saving" (Acts 2:46-47). "On the Saturday night, in our assembly for the breaking of bread, Paul, who was to leave the next day addressed them and went on speaking until midnight . . . (Eutychus incident) . . . He then went upstairs, broke bread and ate, and after much conversation, which lasted until dawn, he departed" (Acts 20:7-11).

These passages describe four distinct parts in the early practice of Holy Communion: the teaching, the fellowship, the breaking of bread, and the prayers. The "teaching" included the reading of Scriptures and the words of the Apostles or prophets that were present. The witness of those who had seen the resurrected Lord was cherished and considered authoritative among the fellowship (cf. Acts 4:33; 5:12-16, 32). The "prayers" referred to in the passages are understood to be the prayers of the Lord's Supper, in remembrance of

Christ. The giving of these prayers was considered as primarily the function of the teachers. The *Didache* states, "The prophets are allowed to give thanks as they want."[4] Later in the development of the Communion liturgy the Lord's Prayer was used in the service.

The term "breaking of bread" is closely related to "fellowship." In Acts 2:42 there is no conjunction between the two terms which indicates their belonging together.[5] Thus it is evident that the "fellowship" (*koinonia*), the "breaking of bread," and "prayers" are integral parts of the Apostolic Communion service. The New Testament agape passages lead us to believe that the fellowship is the Love-feast, and the breaking of bread is the Eucharist of Communion. Breaking of bread always had religious significance in Judaism and Christianity (cf. Luke 24:30; Matt. 5:6; John 6:35, 50). The fact that "breaking of bread" and not "eating bread" is the term used signifies a special religious act. In Acts the term "breaking of bread" became the accepted title of Communion, probably because it was the first official act of the supper.

Many New Testament scholars believe that *koinonia* meant the "communion of believers," and that it referred to a definite part of the worship.[6] A scholar writes, "The concept of corporate being, of fellowship, realized through the presence of Christ, is pushed too much into the background in most present day communion services."[7] The bonded fellowship of the Christian family in the Apostolic period was most real. The words of the Lord became a reality, "Who is my mother? Who are my brothers? and, pointing to the disciples, he said, 'Here are my mother and my brothers. Whoever does the

[4] *Didache* 10.6.

[5] *Kai* is omitted by Westcott and Hort, Alford, Nestle, and Weiss.

[6] Bruce, F. F., *The Acts of the Apostles,* (London: Tyndale Press, 1951), p. 100.

[7] Cullmann, Oscar, *Early Christian Worship,* (London: SCM Press, 1959), p. 18.

will of my heavenly Father is my brother, my sister, my mother' " (Matt. 12:50). The fellowship was more than a social gathering; it was a new creation.

The term, "the Christian fellowship," is clearly defined for our use by Professor William Barclay.[8] The classical Greek use of the term included an association, community, human society, and generous sharing. In secular Greek the term was used to express a business partnership, a marriage, or a man's relationship with God. In the New Testament "koinonia" is used in an embracing sense of the fellowship. The Christian fellowship embraces many meanings: (1) The first meaning of the term is "a sharing of friendship." This is based upon knowing Christ for only those who know Christ can know and be known by each other. (2) The Christian fellowship is practical by way of sharing. This was illustrated in the early Church's collection for the poor of Jerusalem. (3) The fellowship with the family of God includes the fact of partnership. Christians are partners one with another in all of life, in every circumstance. (4) The Christian Communion is always a corporate function, "in the faith." We can't have fellowship alone. (5) The *koinonia* is also "in the spirit." The Christian is alone in the world only in the sense that he is called out from the unbelieving world. The Christian is never alone in this life for he belongs to the fellowship of believers and is in fellowship with God in the Holy Spirit. (6) The Christian fellowship is especially found in Holy Communion, "in Christ." While the Christian has continual fellowship with God through the Holy Spirit, yet supremely in the Eucharist do we have communion in Christ. (7) The Christian fellowship is "with God," for those who live by the light of the truth of the Gospel. "Surely there is no more gracious group of words than this. The Christian shares in the manhood of all men; he shares in the common experience of joy

[8] Barclay, William, *A New Testament Wordbook,* (London: SCM Press, 1955), pp. 71-74.

and tears; he shares in the things divine and in the glory that shall be; and all his life he must be a sharer of all he has, for he knows that his true wealth lies in what he gives away."[9]

From this detailed definition of *koinonia*, Christian fellowship, in the New Testament we understand that it means infinitely more than simple "socialism." To define the Christian fellowship as a free helping of each other's needs is shallowness and an error. To say that the *koinonia* in Acts is a simple sharing of possessions is failing to comprehend the depth of its meaning. The context of fellowship in the book of Acts is "teaching," "breaking of bread," "prayers," and "the saving of souls;" in other words, Holy Communion. Or we might say that the "teaching," "breaking of bread," "prayers" and "the saving of souls" were in the context of *koinonia*, the Christian fellowship. They gathered in private, as a company of Christian brothers, around a supper-table which, in some way, was their Master's table. Here at the Love-feast a person knew his brother and was known as a brother. The fellowship was *among* the brethren, but *in* Christ. The end and purpose of the *koinonia* was not social fellowship, but soul-fellowship with God in Christ through the Holy Spirit.

The Christians of this early time gravitated naturally to the holding of their fellowship in private homes, which were of an informal and intimate kind. Before Pentecost, we find the eleven, with the women and the brothers of Jesus gathered in the upper room, where they resorted with one accord to prayer (Acts 1:12-14). On the day of Pentecost, it was when the disciples were all together seated in a love-fellowship that the Spirit came upon them and they spoke with tongues (Acts 2:1ff.). We read also of the house of Mary, the mother of John Mark, where a number had met for prayer (Acts 1:12).

The *koinonia* of the early Christians is expressed today in the Love-feast of our Holy Communion. Holy Communion is the bond of the Church's fellowship, not only with Christ, but

[9] *Ibid.*

also between its members. When we claim oneness with Christ we are immediately one in the body of Christ, the family of God. There is a brotherhood among all who share like faith, and a unity of the whole company in heaven and earth inherent in Christ. This fact of the brotherhood of believers should not lead one to the false concept of the brotherhood of mankind. Neither should it be interpreted into a glib kind of social fellowship in the Church. This "*fellowship*" *is the Church*! The Church is created out of the oneness of regenerated, newborn creatures of God. The Agape-feast is the practice of this Christian fellowship in Holy Communion.

When Paul speaks of the Church as a "body" of which the head is Christ, he is visualizing the fellowship as gathered together for worship. And it is to be remembered that worship for these early Christians was Holy Communion. It was fellowship at once with Christ the Head and with each other as members of His divine body. Each believer was an actual member of that living body! As they began to realize what this meant at the Love-feast, their faith grew. Paul described the fellowship by the metaphor, "the body of Christ." The metaphor is frequent in Greek language, like a "body-politic," and seems to fit the community of Christians. Paul employs the term in such a corresponding way to the fellowship that it ceased to be metaphor and became symbol, and finally an equation, "ye *are* the body of Christ" (Rom. 12:4). As Paul participated in and beheld the members of Christ in the fellowship partaking of Holy Communion, each functioning and performing his duty, he aptly described it as the "body of Christ."

Among the strongest appeals which early Christians made to the outsider was the human warmth and the solidarity of their fellowship. The fellowship, *koinonia*, of the first Christians and of the body of Christ is vitiated by the "Protestant hour" on Sunday morning. The fulness of the communion-fellowship of the Apostolic period is hardly realized by twentieth-century Christians. We debase the experience of Christian fellowship by formal Church worship and traditions. The Church generally speaks of this "Christian fellowship," but fails to provide the means for its realization. The Love-feast of our Holy Communion is the realization of the bonded fellowship of the Christian faith. Certainly anything less than this in Holy Communion gravely limits the "fellowship," the bonded brotherhood in Jesus Christ and the family of God.

The fellowship of the Christians was evident through the Apostolic period in many regions. In Acts, the twentieth chapter, we learn that Paul was in Asia leading a Christian fellowship twenty-four years after the Last Supper in Jerusalem. It is interesting to note that after many years, in a new land, the place of the gathering was still a private home, an upper room. The service took place at night in a way commemorative of the Last Supper, and also for the very common reason that many of the believers were slaves and could not devote hours during the daytime to worship. The "breaking of bread," the term for Holy Communion, was the heart of the service as recorded by Luke. The occurrence was during the Passover season, and included many hours of teaching by Paul. Considering all of these items, Passover season, breaking of bread, length of service, teaching, and the close fellowship of the brethren, we must conclude that this was an early Christian Love-feast enshrining the Eucharist of Holy Communion. When one reads a more detailed description of the Agape-feast, such as in the *Didache* or in the writings of Tertullian, one can obviously see how the language used in this passage reflects the Love-feast.

The fellowship of the early Christians does have violations. As Christians we tend to idealize the past as all good, and the early Church as our perfect norm. However, it is evident from even a superficial study of the New Testament that there were diversity and division (cf. Acts 15:39; Gal. 2; I Cor.). This is only human and natural, and in no sense disqualifies the essence of Christianity or the reality of the fellowship. The Scriptures do not seek to hide real human life as it is in the world.

Jealousies and divisions existed, as is evidenced in the letter to the Philippians where Paul refers to those who are preaching Christ from "envy and rivalry" (Phil. 1:15-18).

The passages in Corinthians, Jude, and II Peter, concerning the abuses of the Love-feast, might lead one to believe that it was only a source of trouble. However, there is the strong argument from silence that, of the many churches founded in this period, only a few, particularly the Church at Corinth, abused the Love-feast. Paul certainly introduced and taught the Love-feast in all the churches which he founded, and with the exception of Corinth they seemingly practiced it in love, *agape*, and fellowship, *koinonia*.

The impression one receives from all these passages is that the Apostolic Church was a genuine fellowship, bonded together in agape-love. The passage, "With one mind, . . . in exuberant, unaffected joy . . ." characterizes their fellowship. The evidence of their love-fellowship was in the fact that they enjoyed *all* the people's favor. Their faith and worship also had the favor of God, who added daily to the community in salvation. The Love-feast, the fellowship, was practiced and experienced in the Holy Communion of the Apostolic Church. The Love-feast, the Christian *koinonia*, is that bond which binds Christians to each other, and to God.[10]

Another distinguishing characteristic of the Love-feast in Holy Communion during the Apostolic period was the note of "exuberant joy," (*agalliasei*), "unaffected joy." The spiritual exuberance of these early gatherings springs from the resurrection. Their minds and hearts were not so much filled with the memory of the Last Supper or Good Friday as with Easter and the post-resurrection meals. Peter's sermon reveals their experience in post-resurrection *agapai*. "He was put to death by hanging on a tree; but God raised him to life on the third day, and allowed him to appear, not to the whole

[10] Barclay, *op. cit.*, p. 72.

people, but to us, who ate and drank with him after he rose from the dead" (Acts 10:39-41). Certainly the "rejoicing" in these early gatherings, the exhibited exuberance of these early believers could not be confined within the context of the "eucharist" alone. The *koinonia*, the Love-feast, was the natural setting for the expression of joy in the *living* Christ!

The joy was no mere emotional or effervescent thing, but a joy that was always touched with awe, and was kept sober by the adoring of God in Christ. The prayers of the early Christians reflect this adoration. Sometimes a whole chain of historical events is made the object of prayers, or some single event such as the death and resurrection of Christ. The giving of thanks was the predominant motive in early worship, overshadowing both petition and confession.

The habitual use of *eucharistein* in the New Testament, designating thanksgiving prayer, reflects the early Church. The marked predominance of the word *eucharistia* in the New Testament cannot be an accident, when we consider that this word was not only frequent on the lips of Jesus (Matt. 15:36; 26:27; Mark 8:6; 14:23; 22:17), but also in almost every one of Paul's letters (I Cor. 1:4; 10:30; II Cor. 1:11; 4:15; 9:11; Eph. 1:16; 5:4; Phil. 1:3; Col. 1:3, 12; 3:17; I Thess. 3:9; Rom. 14:6). In the Christian faith prayer became personal prayer of thanksgiving; whereas, previously it had been of praise. In Holy Communion both the Love-feast and the eucharistic thanksgiving are experiences of "unaffected joy."

The "fellowship," when in Holy Communion, prays and sings praises, knowing itself to be one with the choir of angels surrounding the throne of God, one with the brethren who have been made perfect, whom the author of the Apocalypse beheld standing before the throne of the Lamb clothed in white robes, offering praise and intercession. The fellowship reached out its arms towards the world; and the joy of its worship on earth was attuned to the majestic joy of the worship above.

The Agape in the Early Church Period

The many Church Fathers left much written material concerning the Agape in the practice of the Church until approximately 400 A.D. The writings of the Church Fathers are highly allegorical with a wide variance of teaching on the same Christian subject. Therefore, the writings of the Church Fathers are considered illustrative and illuminating, but not authoritative concerning a subject like the Agape.[11] The period may be divided into eastern and western for better understanding and convenience of study.

The eastern area of the early Church had two major divisions, Asia and Africa. One of the most important writings from this period is the *Didache*, written not later than 150 A.D.[12] Chapters IX and X of the *Didache* describe the Agape and Eucharist in early Christian worship.[13] Chapter IX refers to the thanksgiving and the Eucharist: "As for 'The Thanksgiving,' give thanks thus; at first for the chalice. . . Let no one eat or drink of your Eucharist, if they have not been baptized in the name of the Lord." Chapter X describes the Love-feast: "After you are filled give thanks. . ." and also the prayers of the service: "As for the prophets, let them give thanks as much as they desire."[14] From these earliest of Christian instructions we understand the Lord's Supper to include the Agape and the Eucharist in the normal pattern of the Apostolic period.

Ignatius is another very early Christian source for the Agape. Ignatius, somewhat like St. Paul, lived at Antioch, from where he journeyed through Asia Minor to Rome to a martyr's death. He wrote three epistles containing twenty-eight references

11 Cullmann, *op. cit.*, p. 85.

12 Vokes, F. E., *The Riddle of the Didache,* (New York: Macmillan, 1938), p. 216.

13 Vokes, *op. cit.*, p. 87.

14 *Didache* ix., 1.5.

to the Agape. He writes, "It is not lawful without the bishop either to baptize or to celebrate a Love-feast."[15]

Alongside Christian fathers was Pliny, Governor of Bithynia, who wrote the famous letter to Trojan in 112 A.D. Pliny complains that he is uncertain about the policy toward Christians, who were spreading rapidly. He then describes their Christian worship: "They met on a stated day before it was light and sang hymns to Christ as God, . . . after which it was their custom to separate, and then reassemble, to eat in common a harmless meal."[16] This letter affirms the fact that the Agape had spread to a very remote corner of a remote province of the Roman Empire and had become established as the component part of the Lord's Supper in the beginning of the second century.

The African Churches also practiced the Agape in the early Church period. Clement of Alexandria and Origen are the sources for the writings concerning the Agape. Clement of Alexandria wrote in "The Instructor": "The agape meals should be simple and frugal."[17] Origen wrote: ". . . and his desire is to slander what is called the agape of the Christians among themselves. . ." about Ellsus who had accused the Christians.[18] From Tertullian's writings the "Apology" is outstanding for the practice of the Agape.[19] From this passage we understand the practice of the Agape in Carthage to involve: (1) a full, real meal, (2) an accepted liturgical order of service in practice, (3) a meal governed by the chastity of Christians, (4) washing of hands after the feast, (5) lighting the lights, (6) singing of sacred songs of original composition.

The fourth-century Church in the east is represented by Chrysostom. He writes, "Rejoice in the Lord with trembling, but how then can one rejoice? Why, by singing hymns,

[15] Ignatius, *Epistle to the Smyraneons,* vii.
[16] Pliny, Book x, Letter xcvii.
[17] Clement of Alexandria, *The Instructor,* 11.1.
[18] Origen, *Contia Celsum.*
[19] Tertullian, *Apology,* Ch. 39.

making prayers, introducing psalms in the place of those low songs. Thus will Christ also be at our table, and will fill the whole feast with blessing."[20]

The abuses continued, however, until the Emperor Justinian II in 692 A.D. summoned an Oecumenical Synod to meet in the Trullon Hall at Constantinople where Canon 74 was read forbidding Love-feasts within the Church.

The Agape continued, however, in different sections of the eastern Church. The Syrian, Armenian, and Georgian Churches practised the Agape from the teachings of the early Church. The Abyssinian Church continued the practice of the Agape for some centuries. The Albigenses in the west also had a form of the Agape in practice. The Armenians were practicing the Agape many centuries later.[21] Another very genuine practice of the Agape from the Apostolic period is among the Christians of St. Thomas. These Christians have continued a church colony at Madras in southern India.[22]

The eastern section of the early Church also carried the Gospel into Bohemia and Bulgaria. As the Church in the east grew, the Roman powers tried to coerce them into Roman liturgy and the Latin language. The Bohemians consistently refused to acquiesce to the Roman power. Each time the Roman See tried to conquer the eastern brethren there arose strong men to defend the faith. This was the background of John Huss and Jerome of Prague. The great principle of the Hussite movement was that whatever in government, doctrine, and worship could not be demonstrated in Scripture should be implicitly rejected.[23]

In the midst of the larger movement of the Christian faith there emerged a fellowship known as the "unitas Fratrum," the

[20] Chrysostom, *Homily on Romans,* 24.

[21] Coynbeare, "Agape," *Encyclopedia Britannica,* (London: 1911 ed.), Vol. I, p. 340.

[22] Thorston, Herbert, ed., *Catholic Encyclopedia,* New York, Vol. XIV, p. 658.

[23] Cole, *op. cit.,* p. 271.

League of Brethren.[24] They practiced the Pedilavium, the Agape, and the Eucharist, placing emphasis upon Christian living rather than creeds. Personal faith in the crucified Savior constituted the chief foundation for the Brethren, and Scripture was the only rule of faith.

The "League of Brethren" are the link in the chain from the Apostolic and Church Father period to the Reformation period, through men like Wyclif, John Huss, Count Zinzendorf, and even John Wesley. Wesley's conversion through the Moravian Brethren is well known. The influence of the Moravian Brethren doctrine is evident in Wesley's early ministry. John Wesley once taught the Agape "in order to increase in them a grateful sense of all His mercies . . . that they might together eat bread, as the ancient Christians did, 'with gladness and singleness of heart.'" At these Love-feasts the food was only a plain cake and water.[25] In his Journal he wrote: "My brother Charles was present at our Love-feast in Fetter Lane, with about sixty of our brethren. They remained instant in prayer . . . and exceeding joy. . ."[26] Only conflict of the Methodist movement with the Moravian movement caused Wesley to discontinue the Agape.

The "western" Church's practice of the Agape was never as extensive as it was in the east. The Apostle Paul did teach the Agape in the churches he founded in Europe. However, with the ascending power of the Roman Church the Agape was lost in the ecclesiastical hierarchy of the later centuries. An early western Christian apologist Minucius Felix wrote in reply to the charges that the Christian Agape was licentious: "We hold our feast not only modestly but soberly also. We have no desire for luxurious banquets,

[24] Wilhelm, J., "Bohemian Brethren," *Catholic Encyclopedia,* Vol. II, p. 616.

[25] Curnock, Nehemiah, ed., *The Journal of John Wesley,* (London: Kelly Company), Vol. III, p. 168.

[26] Curnock, Nehemiah, ed., *The Journal of John Wesley,* Vol. II, pp. 121, 122.

neither do we protract the feast by strong drink, but we temper our rejoicings with a seriousness, a chaste conversation, and a body more chaste."[27]

The direction and practice of western Christianity in the fourth century was influenced by Augustine, Ambrose, and Jerome. However, none of them has much to say concerning the Agape. Augustine at one point writes: "We have not turned their sacrifices into Agapes, but we have come to understand that notable sacrifice of which I spoke just now, at which the Lord said, 'I will have mercy, for our love feasts feed the poor.'"[28]

An interesting phenomenon in the practice of the Agape in the early Church is the Agape in the catacombs. Often this is overlooked as the real common-life practice of the Church. In the hundreds of miles of underground corridors the Christian worshippers had a city of their own. It was here during the days of persecution that they assembled to "break bread" and hold their Love-feasts. Here they wrote on the tombs and walls their faith and life in frescos.[29] A number of frescos have been discovered which portray seven people at a Love-feast. The feast seems to have consisted of fish and loaves. These paintings probably depict the feeding of the seven on the shore of Lake Tiberias by the Lord. It is significant that during the period of pagan hate and Roman persecution these early Christians in Rome had an oasis of love and peace. The real purpose of the Agape is fulfilled in the lives of these Christians who are bonded together in love.

The survey of the early Church period in both eastern and western sections of Christianity is conclusive in affirming the practice of the Agape. When then was it discontinued in the predominant practice of the Church? First, the Agape became abused when it moved out of the holy Passover background

[27] Minucius, Felix, *Octavius,* 31.5.
[28] Augustine, *Epistle to Aurelius,* 22.4.
[29] Northcote, J. Spencer, and Brownlow, W. R., *Roma Sotterranea,* (London: Longmans, 1879), p. 73.

into pagan festal practices. Second, the Church grew "amazingly fast" and the original house-to-house Agape became impossible. Third, the Roman government became suspicious of the "fraternity" of the Agape and its social power. Fourth, growing ecclesiasticism excluded the "common" Agape. It was also decreed that bishops be present to direct the Agape, and as the Church grew this became impossible. Fifth, great cathedrals were being built for "public" worship which did not lend themselves to Agapes. The simplicity of the Agape was irreconcilable with solemn splendor and stately offices of a Gothic or a Byzantine building. Sixth, "In the east we hear more about the Lord's Supper than we do in the west. Doubtless the small country churches found it much easier to keep up the custom of meeting for an Agape than the larger town churches, and in the east Christianity generally spread out to the countryside much earlier than the west."[30]

The good that the service of Agape left on the early Church period is both implicit in the lives of the believers and explicit in the life of the Church. The Agape was the strong practical means that brought love and brotherhood to the social aspects of the early Church. This was the means whereby master and slave could come as one and Paul could write to Philemon concerning Onesimus. Many are called "slaves" but at the communion of Agape, all were brethren in Christ Jesus. It was the Agape that struck the first real blow at slavery.

It was from the early practice of Agape that Christian charity began with determined direction. "Christianity for the first time made charity a rudimentary virtue, giving it a leading place in the moral life. . ."[31] The Agape was the center of help for children, widows, and helpless souls. In fact, out of this rudimentary virtue came houses of mercy, missions, orphanages, and public hospitals.[32]

[30] Dix, *op. cit.*, p. 85.

[31] Lecky, William, *History of European Morals,* (London: Longmans, Green Co., 1902), Vol. II, pp. 78ff.

[32] *Ibid.*

The good that surrounds the Agape of the early Church, even with the few spots of abuses, declares its value and validity. During the darkest hours of Christian persecution the Agape was the means of expressing loving care. Tertullian, in speaking of Christians in prison, says that the spirit and flesh do not lose anything by being put into prison, because of the care of the Church and the Agape of the brethren.[33] St. Chrysostom writes: "The Agape is a custom most beautiful and most beneficial, for it was a supporter of love, a solace of poverty, and a discipline of humility."[34]

From Catacombs to Cathedrals

In the fourth century, the Diocletian persecution (303-313 A.D.), followed by the Roman Emperor's acceptance of the Christian faith as his personal religion, brought immense change to the Church. The immensity of the change in the external situation of the Church and its effect upon the character and communion of the Church is almost impossible for us to perceive fully. The sudden change in the circumstances of the Church in the fourth century is unparalleled in the history of the Church. Almost overnight the status of Christians changed from a fellowship, worshiping in semisecrecy against the political law, to a state religion shared by the Emperor and society. They were no longer "hunted-down" for persecution, but "hunted-up" for patronage. The Christian Church was to live no longer in a hostile world, but in a society whose conscience and laws it was directing. Following the Diocletian persecution the transformation of the Church from a "fellowship" to a "religion" was rapidly completed within a decade.

The change was a permanent change, not a respite between persecutions as they had sometimes experienced in the past. Christianity was now lawful and the full weight and authority

[33] Tertullian, *Ad Martyrs,* Chapter 11.
[34] Chrysostom, *Homily on I Corinthians xl.*

of the Emperor was behind it. Rome had always made p
visions for religious worship, and now it was the Christian faith that was to receive its favor. The Emperor himself built nine new churches in Rome. They included the richly furnished cathedral of Rome, St. Peter on the Vatican, and St. Paul beside the road to Ostia over the tombs of the two Roman Apostles. Other prominent persons soon followed the Emperor's example. Constantine built magnificent church buildings at Ostia, Naples, Albano, Carthage, Jerusalem, Bethlehem, Mamre, Antioch, Thessalonica, and scores of other places in the provinces, besides a number in the new capital at Constantinople. The whole Mediterranean world soon became the scene of new Christian basilicas. Even in remote areas and in the countrysides, many, many new Christian buildings were built and dedicated. The furnishings were as generous as the buildings themselves.

St. Peter's Church in Rome is an example of the rich furnishings used in the basilicas of this period.[35] The vaulting of the apse was plated with pure gold. There was a great cross of solid gold, and the altar was of silver-gilt set with 400 precious stones. There was a large dish for receiving the offerings of the people, and a jewelled "tower" with a dove of pure gold brooding upon it, probably a vessel for the reserved sacrament. There were five silver potens for administration, three gold and jewelled chalices and twenty of silver; two golden flagons and five silver ones for receiving the oblations of wine. There was a jewelled golden "censer," perhaps a standing burner for perfumed oil or spices rather than what we understand by the word. Before the Apostle's tomb was a great golden corona of lights and four large standard candlesticks wrought with silver medallions depicting scenes from the Acts of the Apostles. The nave lit with thirty-two candelabra of silver and the aisles by thirty more. These

[35] Dix, Gregory, *The Shape of the Liturgy,* (Westminster: Dacre Press, 1955), p. 310.

furnishings of St. Peter's are not exceptional, but a true example of all churches of this size and period. The smaller churches were just as richly furnished in a proportionate way.

In this new world of glitter and freedom the "fellowship," the "ecclesia," experienced significant changes not only in its form but in its faith. There was the immediate danger of compromise of faith and practice, and the more subtle changes not perceptible to themselves or the historians. Generally, the earlier standards were no longer adhered to nor made a test of faith. Christians had to decide where the line existed between courteous social custom and disloyalty to Christ. The pagan cults were still very much in evidence and practice. For instance, the Christian guest knew that much of the hospitality was offered in the honor of some heathen god; and often these gods were the very same ones under which the previous Christian generation had been persecuted and martyred!

Another far-reaching change in the Church of this period was a change in leadership. The memory of the Apostles and early Christian prophets had faded into a distant background. The previous generation of Christian leaders who had been grounded in the faith was to a large extent martyred or dispersed during the Diocletian persecution. The men and women who had suffered persecution for their Christian faith were no longer predominant in the leadership of the Church. Eusebius of Caesarea stood for the bygone order. He had been a leader during the terrible Palestinian persecution and so feared heathenism chiefly as a persecuting power that he was lulled into security when Constantine adopted Christianity. The new order of leadership was represented by Athanasias, who spent his life and ministry defending the faith against the more subtle dangers arising. Crowds of heathen followed the Emperor with a facile profession of religion on their lips and a traditional attachment to heathenism in their hearts. Overnight, as it were, a new generation of leaders was now forming the character of the Church in this new situation.

The Christian faith was being defined by church creeds rather than by Apostolic authority.

Christian worship quickly changed in pattern to conform to the new rich cathedrals in which it was now being practiced. The internal character of the Church tended to conform to the external circumstances of the ornate cathedrals. Certainly it is evident that the intimate worship in homes and catacombs could no longer function in the large cathedrals. The more elaborate public worship brought with it formalism. Ecclesiastical worship of the Church often took the place of a sincere surrender of the heart and will. The glitter of the cathedral furnishings outshone the glory of Christ in the lives of His fellowship. It was at this point in history when the Church became known as a building rather than a *koinonia*, or *ecclesia*, the body of Christ. Christianity tended to become "churchism."

The fellowship, the Love-feast, no longer fitted in this new environment. In fact, these new basilicas excluded the Agape by their very design. *It certainly is no minor fact that the decline of the practice of the Love-feast paralleled the rise of the cathedral!* Cathedrals inevitably tended toward liturgical services of formality, rather than friendly intimate fellowships of the previous Christian generations. Such plain practices as the Pedilavium and the Love-feast were incongruous in this new church splendor and consequently faded from the practice of the Church. The rise of this new churchism which paralleled the fall of many practices of the early Church is generally minimized in church history; however, it is striking and highly significant. A predominance of Christian theology was formed in this new church period and most certainly bears its stamp. The doctrines were supremely stated in an orthodoxy that is basic to this day. However, the organization of the church itself and its practices, such as Holy Communion, received their form and image from this new churchism, rather than from the Apostolic faith and order.

The church became reconciled to time. The expectation of

the *parousia* faded. With the end of persecution came the end of the predominant emphasis in eschatological teaching. The eschatological emphasis in the Eucharist also faded. Holy Communion gradually ceased to mean the joyous fact of the resurrection and became a silent sacrament of the Church. The Communion, which was once offered only to those who lived their faith, or was administered to a brother before martyrdom, was now being offered to anyone who was officially baptized. The service of Holy Communion came under the exclusive control of ecclesiastical leadership. Private worship surrendered to Church ecclesiology.

This does not imply that it was ever intended that the "fellowship" remain in the homes or catacombs; nor are we implying that today we must return to the primitive circumstances to be a real church. Christian equipment must fit the needs of the day, and the soul of man always needs the beauty of worship. Slovenly worship is every bit as much a sin as slovenly faith. However, the sudden change from private to public worship, from persecution to privilege, changed the internal character of the *ecclesia*. Also, the change from catacomb to cathedral resulted in a completely different form of worship. The Holy Communion in this new period of churchism was reduced to a eucharistic sacrament. Love-feasts and the Pedilavium were discontinued, not for reasons of Christian doctrine, but for reasons of society and the ecclesiastical church. The Biblical and spiritual basis for the practice of the Love-feast has not changed.

The Love-Feast and Christian Doctrine

The practice of the Love-feast as one component part of Communion is based on historic Christian tradition and Christian doctrine. The Love-feast was instituted and practiced conjointly with the Eucharist and the Pedilavium. It was at the Last Supper where the Lord washed the disciples' feet and where Jesus took bread and the cup and related it to His broken body and shed blood on the Cross. It is not inconceivable that Jesus could have chosen another time and place to institute the sacrament of Communion if the Eucharist was to be the only means of communing. However, he ordained the Last Supper as the setting for the institution of the "Feet-washing," the "Love-feast," and the "Eucharist" in Holy Communion. Thus we regard it as a significant institution and accept it in faith and practice.

When the Love-feast is accepted in faith and practice today, it is the rich symbolic means of teaching three central doctrines of the Church. The practice of the Love-feast dramatizes the doctrine of (1) the full victory of Christ, (2) the foretaste of heavenly fellowship in the marriage supper of the Lamb and His Church, and (3) the family of God. The very soul of the Love-feast will be set forth in these three catagories.

THE FULL VICTORY OF CHRIST – From the beginning, Christianity was a faith of triumphant hope, a "resurrection faith," a faith based on the conviction that love was stronger than death and could not be holden of death, but must rise from death to life eternal. No Gospel of mere renunciation and the Cross, however noble the Messiah, could have the tremendous power of spiritual appeal which the fellowship has ever since proved itself to possess. The Lord instituted the Love-feast as a means whereby His joyful triumph through all ensuing ages could be conjoined with His sacrificial death. The death without the triumph in Christian worship and Holy Communion is incomplete and tragic. Just as the bread and cup symbolize the broken body and shed blood of Christ, so the Love-feast symbolizes and expresses the joy of the triumphant resurrection.

Christ's victory is an important element of the Holy Communion that is largely overlooked and ignored. The theologian Jeremias writes, "The alternative, the eucharist a reenactment of the death of Jesus or an eschatological feast of joy, must not be decided exclusively one way or the other, for the two are closely inter-related. Jesus himself celebrated the Eucharist singing the jubilant psalm of thanksgiving which gives praise to Him who leads His Messiah through chastening to the opened door of salvation."[36] The Last Supper was not only a time of anticipating the Cross, but also the resurrection beyond the Cross. "I shall not die, but live," was the heart of the closing Psalms probably sung by the Lord in the upper room (Ps. 118:17).

The triune Holy Communion, including the Love-feast, is the exact service to symbolize the rejoicing deliverance. The one-phase eucharistic type of Communion practiced by many branches of the Church is an insufficient way to symbolize the ultimate truth of the Christ, "I lay my life down, that I might take it up again" (cf. 116-118; John 10:17). To demonstrate clearly that the Last Supper was not simple tragedy, consider the hymn of praise, Psalm 113-118, which was probably used throughout the evening of the Last Supper by the Lord and His disciples (cf. Matt. 26:30).

"Hallelujah, Praise ye the Lord" (Ps. 113:1) was the invocation at the Last Supper. "Joyousness" was "commanded" by the law for the Passover. The participants of the Passover sang the hymn of praise which included the praise of God, the glories of the exodus, the sovereignty of God, the deliverance from death by the power of God, the mercies of God, and the jubilant thanksgiving to God.[37] Of course the service was serious, with the presence of the traitor and the impending Cross. However, the perspective of the Last Supper must always contain the strong ray of glad hope in history's dark night. The Love-feast of the triune Holy Communion provides the setting of both praises of the old

[36] Jeremias, *op. cit.*, p. 174.
[37] Cf. Kirkpatrick, A. F., *Psalms,* (London: Cambridge University Press, 1910), pp. 7ff.

Passover and the "exuberant joy" of the early Lord's Supper on the Lord's Day.

Jesus and His disciples celebrated the Last Supper singing the jubilant hymns of praise, deliverance, and thanksgiving to the Father who leads the Suffering Servant through death (cf. Ps. 23:4) to resurrected life. All feasts were joyous occasions, but this one had added significance because this was the one that would rend the curtain in two and open the door of salvation.

The Holy Communion is the solemn proclamation of the Lord's death; but it is also the familiar intercourse of Jesus abiding in the soul, as a friend who enters in and sups with a friend. The Love-feast fulfills the past as the true and secret manna. It also looks forward to the future beyond the end of time, as a mysterious anticipation of the final judgment of God, a tasting of the powers of the world to come. It foreshadows the exultant welcome of his own at the second coming (Rev. 19:7-9).

The place of the Love-feast in Christian worship in the contemporary world needs little deliberation. In a world beset with the fear of destruction, our faith in the Almighty Deliverer needs joyful proclamation. In a secular society that is frantic in seeking vain happiness, the Christian faith must express its eternal happiness in joy and praise. The Eucharist proclaims the death of Christ; the Love-feast, the victorious new life in Christ; and the Pedilavium, the cleansing from sin. The end of Christian sacrifice is not death, but life. The Apostles celebrated the Lord's Supper in remembrance, not of the Last Supper, but of the post-resurrection meals where the victorious Christ revealed that He was not dead, but alive!

The church's celebration of Holy Communion takes place with mixed emotion: sadness in that our sins crucified the Savior, but also gladness that He bore them on the Cross and buried death once and for all in the tomb. The last act of the Lord in the upper room was the singing of the hymn of praise. The Love-feast today is the symbolic means in Holy Communion of acting out Christ's triumphant deliverance. Halleujah!

THE FORETASTE OF THE MARRIAGE SUPPER OF THE LAMB AND THE CHURCH – The marriage supper of the Lamb and the Bride, the Church, is perfectly symbolized in Christian worship by the Love-least. Just as there is no other adequate way in the Christian fellowship to express the family of God and the full victory of God, so there is no other satisfying way to symbolize the consummation of Christ and His Bride. The interpretation of the Lord's Supper would not be complete without the concept of future Messianic redemption. Faith itself will become sight; hope will become fruition; and love, the eternal, abiding love of God will be an eternal feast. It is this love that shines through the Love-feast as a symbol and type, and gives it an abiding glory.[38]

The Lord's ministry in the Gospel of John begins with the significant sign at the marriage supper at Cana, which takes place on the "third day." One day later in His ministry, someone asked him, "Sir, are only a few to be saved. . . When once the Master of the house has got up and locked the door, you may stand outside the knock, . . . But he will repeat . . . Out of my sight all of you, you and your wicked ways: There will be wailing and grinding of teeth, when you see Abraham, Isaac, and Jacob, and all the prophets, in the Kingdom of God, and yourselves thrown out, from east and west people will come, from north and south, for the feast in the Kingdom of God" (Luke 13:22-30). On the eve of the Cross Jesus speaks to His disciples, "You are the men who have stood firmly by me in my times of trial; and now I vest in you the kingship which my Father vested in me; you shall eat and drink at my table in my kingdom and sit on thrones as judges of the twelve tribes of Israel" (Luke 22:28-30). There-

[38] Yoder, C. F., *op. cit.*, p. 369.

fore, in the upper room, the Love-feast was inaugurated and pointed forward to the consummation, when symbol and foretaste would at last give place to the Messianic fulfillment in the eternal Kingdom of God.

The Revelation of John proclaims, "Alleluia! The Lord our God, sovereign over all, has entered on his reign. Exult and shout for joy and do him homage, for the wedding day of the Lamb has come! His bride has made herself ready, and for her dress she has given fine linen, clean and shining. Then the angel said to me, Write this; Happy are those who are invited to the wedding-supper of the Lamb" (Rev. 19:7-9)!

The Jewish Passover was the symbol standing between the Egyptian deliverance and the coming Messiah. The Love-feast is the symbol standing between the Messiah's passion-resurrection and His *parousia!* The Church, the New Israel, already passed from death to life through faith in Him, still waits for the redemption of the body, when the final robes of righteousness shall be put on forever!

The Love-feast of the triune Holy Communion expresses in rich symbolic form the Father's *agape* in the hearts of His family, Christ's victory in the resurrection, and Christ's consummation of His Kingdom. In the Love-feast we gain great confidence, looking forward to the time when we shall be with Christ at the heavenly feast and worship Him with joy and gladness forever and ever. The Communion liturgy of the Moravian Brethren ends with the invitation: "Till he come – to the great Supper at which, in banqueting hall of the consummation, His Bride will behold Him closely. Come, Lord Jesus! The Bride calls!"

THE FAMILY OF GOD – The analogy of the family is prominent in the New Testament Scriptures. The interpretation of *agape* to mean "fatherliness" in the vertical direction, and "brotherliness" in the horizontal direction, must of course together mean the family of God. Without doubt,

Paul regarded the name of Father as the particular Christian name for God. In fact, the very center of the Gospel is that God is our Father and that the way is open whereby we may be received into His sonship (Rom. 8:14-17).

The earliest name for the human side of the "fellowship of love" was "the brotherhood," and the phrase "the whole brotherhood throughout the world" appears as an early name for the Church Universal. The evidence of this brotherhood in the early Church is in the writings of Tertullian: "They are angry with us because we call one another brethren." He also writes, "It is the exercise of this noblest sort of love that leads many to put a brand on us, 'See!' they say, 'how these men love one another . . . and how ready they are even to die for one another.' "[39] The crux of the Christian Gospel is that by faith in the Cross of the only begotten Son we become adopted sons into the family circle of God. The brotherhood of Christians is as real as the fatherhood of God.

The brotherhood of believers is an imperative in the Christian faith: ". . . no one who does not do right is God's child, nor is anyone who does not love his brother. For the message you have heard from the beginning is this: that ye should love one another" (I John 3:10, 11). Further in the same passage is the imperative, "This is his command, to give our allegiance to his Son Jesus Christ and love one another as he commanded" (I John 3:23). In the same epistle John writes, "If God thus loved us, dear friends, we in turn are bound to love one another" (I John 4:11). Paul writes to the churches of Galatia, "For the whole law can be summed up in a single commandment: love your neighbor as yourself" (Gal. 5:14). The *agape* love was central to the Thessalonica Church: "About love for our brotherhood you need no words of mine, for you are yourselves taught by God to love one another, and you are in fact practising this rule of love towards all your fellow-Christians throughout Macedonia" (I

[39] Tertullian, *Apology*, 39.

Thess. 4:9). Many more passages lend to the truth that loving our brother is a central truth in the Christian faith (John 5:42; 14:21; 15:12, 17; Rom. 13:8, 9; Eph. 5:2; Jas. 2:8; I Pet. 1:22; 2:17; I John 4:17-21; II John 5).

The fellowship of love, the Christian love of one's brother, is nowhere more richly or fully realized in Christian worship than in the Love-feast. Eating together in all time and history has been a symbol of bonded friendship and love. In the Scriptures are many examples of eating together as a pledge of friendship and love. The meetings of Melchizedek and Abraham (Gen. 14:18), of family events such as marriages, of birthdays, and of friends are examples of the symbol of bonded love in table fellowship (Gen. 14:17, 18; Judg. 14:10; Gen. 40:20). The concept of the Love-feast in the day of our Lord was that the table companions are bound into bonded love. The Love-feast is a fellowship that includes obligations, the violation of which is a crime (Ps. 41:9). As members of the family of God our obligation is not only to our heavenly Father, but also to our Christian brother. The "obligation" is transformed from duty to privilege by the *agape* of God.

The concept of the family of God in the Love-feast of Holy Communion embodies other Christian doctrine. The Christian fellowship is based upon the fact that through redemption we are "no more servants but sons" (Gal. 4:7). Paul described this new relationship to God that is characterized by the Christian fellowship in several ways. First of all, we have greater "informality" with the Father: "In Him we have access to God with freedom, in the confidence born of trust in Him" (Eph. 3:12). We also have the greater "graciousness" of our sins and failures in this new Christian fellowship. What we know from our Christian experience is that God receives us on a family basis, rather than on a judicial basis. Our heavenly Father deals with us not on a legal basis, but on a parental basis: "We are not under law, but under grace" (Rom. 4:14). The Love-feast of our Holy Communion embraces and expresses these central truths of the faith. The Love-feast, with the Pedilavium and the Eucharist, expresses the essence of the total Christian faith. The triune Holy Communion is the full expression of Christianity.

The Love-Feast In Present Practice

The question is asked, however, whether the Love-feast is still a meaningful symbol in an age of science and space? Is it relevant to the present Christian era, or has the practice of the Christian faith and worship developed to a point that deletes its use in Holy Communion? Is it ordained of God or is it "myth" that should be distinguished and discarded from the Christian kerygma?

First of all in answer, we would suggest that there is reason to believe that table-fellowship will never go out of "style"! It is as contemporary today as in the day of our Lord. Love-fellowship transcends time and history in everyday life. Therefore, as a means used in Christian worship, it can't honestly be discarded as mythological or out-of-date. It is true that our world has changed in many ways. "Our contemporary world has been telescoped by travel and communication: Moscow, London, New York, Sydney, Peking have become almost suburbs of one another. Many of the old barriers which maintained the fabric of international, political, social, and economic life have been broken down."[40] The caste system has been abolished and, therefore, an outcast has access to law and justice. The world has become a community – in a sense.

In a physical and geographical sense the world has been telescoped together, but in a spiritual sense the people of the world are chasms apart. In one sense the old caste-systems have been broken down and, therefore, people are free to choose; yet in another sense they are bound by a much more subtle imprisonment. Our contemporary world divides

[40] McIntyre, John, *In the Love of God,* (London: Collins, 1962), p. 119.

people into private cliques and clubs, into where and how we live. This type of separation is more sophisticated, but just as severe. In the contemporary world that tends more and more to metropolitan areas, people become isolated in "housing developments" not knowing the neighbor across the hall or across the way. The cement and steel of the modern world are just as hard to overcome as the Great Wall of the ancient world. In a world where people are constantly moving to new places and new homes, there exists the hard truth that neighbors do not know one another. Politically and economically the world has been telescoped into a "suburb," but socially and spiritually people remain strangely separated.

Modern transportation is a fact, but it is more often used to take people away than bring them together. Rapid transit tends to take people away from the fellowship of the Church, rather than bring them together in the love of the Christian family. And even among those who are in church, isn't it true that they are often worshiping as strangers in the same pew? Physical and geographical proximity are no guarantee that there is spiritual proximity.

The Church has become institutional to such an extent that the individual is over-shadowed into oblivion. This cold truth would suggest paraphrasing Jesus' words to read, "Is man made for the Church, or is the Church made for man?" The "fellowship of the saint" is a grand pulpit phrase, but hardly a reality in the pew. Therefore, the Love-feast is as fitting and needful a symbol in Christian worship and experience as in the day of our Lord. The modern Christian needs to be bonded into the Agape-love, the fellowship (*koinonia*) of the early Apostolic Church.

The gregarious nature of man demands fellowship, and the spiritual man demands spiritual fellowship. James Mill is once quoted as suggesting a somewhat notorious way of reforming the Christian Church: "Sunday must be retained as a day of rest, with just sufficient amusement to promote cheerfulness rather than profane merriment. And a conjoint meal on Sunday would have the happiest effects, being a renewal of the Agape-feast of the early Church."

The end of the Diocletian persecution brought the end of private Christian worship in a home where the Communion was given secretly under the penalty of death. Fierce persecution and simple worship were changed to political patronage in less than a decade. The Church came up out of the catacombs and down from its upper room to "Main Street." Lights and incense, golden chalices and jewelled altars – that was how the survivors of the Diocletian persecution worshipped at the Holy Communion. It is almost inconceivable how quickly the *ecclesia* could change their form of worship from hidden candlelight to glittering candelabra, from improvised altar furniture to precious inlaid altar furnishings. *The wooden cross of Christ was exchanged for the great, golden, jewel-studded crosses of the Roman Church.*

This exchange has continued through the centuries and today the Church offers only the cold symbols of Church buildings and gold crosses for Christian love-fellowship. People of the world have come to believe that "The Church" is a building. Lonely people of the Christian faith, and the world, are seeking warm love and the Church offers cold worship services. Unclaimed people are seeking to be claimed into the family of Christ. In a word, people are ever seeking warm love and the Church is ever offering cold crosses.

Certainly the Love-feast is needed in Christian worship today to bring together Christ's family. The Love-feast is the dramatized way for each Christian to know that he is in the family of love. All Christians share in the singular cup of salvation. Holy Communion has a double reference, vertical and horizontal. Christians are bound to their brethren as they are bound to their Christ, by "Agape." The world is awaiting the practice of the Agape-feast in the Church Universal.

5

The Eucharist

We have come to the very heart of Holy Communion, the Eucharist. But what words can be employed to plumb the depths and ascend the heights of this sacramental symbol. All of our learning and most accurate teachings are but glimpses; all of our understanding is but a flash from the surface of its meaning. Whatever is proposed as the soul of this sacramental symbol, it is with the understanding that there is much more that should be said. However, we aspire to obtain the best spiritual understanding with the promise of God that we are nearer the eternal truth by what we affirm than by what we deny. May we always remember that what seems so difficult if approached as a pure intellectual problem has been clear in the hearts of Christians in all generations. Christ does not address the reason of man in the celebration of the Eucharist, but the highest aspiration of our spiritual being. The Holy Communion of man with God in the Eucharist has brought the sense of Christ to all generations of Christians.

Christianity is the divine drama of love, "For God so loved the world"; with action, "that he gave his only begotten

Son"; with reaction, "that whosoever believeth in him"; and with consummation, "should not perish but have everlasting life." The Eucharist is the "action" in this eternal drama of love, the point of the plot. The love story begins before history, "The Lamb of God slain before the foundation of the world" (Rev. 13:8), and shall be consummated beyond the end of history. Between this alpha and omega the action of the love story runs along a "terrestrial track,"[1] firmly nailed down in history, nailed to the Cross. The Cross is the clue to the whole drama of divine love, the key to the mystery of the nature of the love of God and the sin of man and their relationship. The Eucharist is the enacted symbolic drama of divine love in the Christian faith performed repeatedly that the love may be flamed into the faith of eternal life.

The Church perpetually reconstitutes in symbolic action the Cross in the Eucharist. The famous statement of C. H. Dodd summarizes the truth, "At each Eucharist service we are there; we are in the night in which He was betrayed, at Golgotha, before the empty tomb on Easter day, and in the upper room where He appeared; and we are at the moment of His coming, with angels and archangels and all the company of heaven, in the twinkling of an eye at the last trump."[2]

Eucharist has become the technical term used in the Christian faith to denote three things: the prayer of thanksgiving and consecration, the elements of the bread and cup, and the sacramental rite of the bread and cup within Holy Communion. The term *eucharist* is the simple direct translation of the Greek word, *he eucharistia*, meaning "the thanksgiving." The eucharistic thanksgiving of Christian communion is from the specific giving of thanks in prayer over the bread and the cup by Jesus at the Last Supper (Mark

[1] Baillie, D. M., *The Theology of the Sacraments,* (London: Faber and Faber, 1961), p. 56.

[2] Dodd, C. H., *The Apostolic Preaching and its Developments,* (London: Hodder and Stoughton, 1944), p. 94.

14:23; Matt. 26:27; Luke 22:19; I Cor. 11:24). The New Testament Greek term is related to the Old Testament word, *berakah*, the Jewish blessing to God over the food and the drink.[3] To give thanks was synonymous with blessing in Jewish thought. It is in this sense that the term was used by Christ in the Last Supper, and by the apostles in the early Church's Lord's Supper. In the new setting of post-resurrection Lord's Supper, the "thanksgiving" had specific reference to the Lord Jesus Christ.

The earliest description and concept of the Eucharist in the infant Church is that of Justin, A.D. 155. "The president . . . sends up praise and glory to the Father of all things through the name of the Son and the Holy Ghost, and makes thanksgiving (*eucharistian*) at some length that we have been made worthy of these things by Him. And when he has finished the prayers and thanksgiving, all the laity present shout assent saying Amen . . . And when the president has eucharistised and the people have shouted assent. . . ."[4]

In the triune Holy Communion service, the Eucharist is the climaxing part, the solemnizing symbol for which the Pedilavium and the Agape have been preparing the communicant. The three component parts are conjoined in such a way to bring Holy Communion between God and man. The interrelation of the component parts of the triune Communion service are demonstrated by Jesus boldly inserting "This is my body," before the main meal; and "This is my blood of the new covenant, shed for many" after the meal. At these two important junctions, before and after the paschal meal, the bread and cup sayings were instituted, together with the whole sacred service of cleansing and feasting. In the setting of the Passover, Jesus directs the disciples that hereafter the original meaning of the Passover has been transcended in Himself.

[3] Cf. Chapter II.
[4] Justin, *Apology,* 1,65.

The Christian faith has never questioned the fact that the Old Covenant has been transcended by the New Covenant, but the way it is celebrated in the eucharistic sacrament has fostered many questions. The sayings of Jesus Christ concerning the Eucharist are in a sense so plain that it tends towards a materialism, transubstantiation. Yet Christ and the Holy Scriptures make plain that human language can not fully or precisely define spiritual truth. Perhaps it is nearest the truth to say that because this spiritual mystery is more true than plain, many have formed doctrines and churches to their own concepts and fancies, and then have found their teaching more plain than true.[5] A glimpse of the soul of the sacramental symbol can be had only by studying the New Testament passages. After the study of the Scriptural passages the author shall seek to elucidate the teaching of the Eucharist within several major categories that have been predominant in Christian teaching.

The Eucharistic Texts

THE SAYINGS OVER THE BREAD. The Gospels are the world's masterpieces of brevity. Each word is measured in meaning and must be carefully regarded in the context and interpreted by the systematic whole of Scripture. Therefore, the words, "This is my body" can be understood only in the context, "As they were eating he took bread, and when he had blessed, he brake it, and gave to them. . ." Also we must remind ourselves that the Last Supper is in the shadow of the Passover and the feast of Unleavened Bread. The Gospel accounts in their succinct style do not record how Jesus as leader taught the disciples concerning the paschal lamb; however, He undoubtedly attached it to the sacrificial significance of His own death. On His journey to Jerusalem for this feast of Passover He foretells His death and resurrection for the third time, and answers His disciples, "The Son of man came

[5] Cf. Gore, *op. cit.*, p. 155.

not to be served, but to serve, and to surrender his life a ransom for many" (Mark 10:45). Another glimpse of how Jesus regarded His sacrificial death may be seen from the Epistle of Peter, "as of a lamb without mark or blemish" (I Pet. 1:19). Peter may well have learned this divine truth directly from Jesus, even at the Last Supper. The meaning of this reference is that Jesus taught the meaning of His approaching death as a sacrifice of atoning efficacy, and likened Himself to the Passover lamb.[6]

"Take ye" directs the disciples to eat and suggests more than the invitation associated with the common practice of breaking bread. The disciples are instructed to eat with the new interpretation of His life and sacrificial death. The disciples needed the clear command of Christ, even with all His previous teaching during His ministry and during the Last Supper concerning the Lamb of God. This is indeed a modern parable for us today.

"This" refers to the bread which has just been broken, and not to Christ himself. "This – my body" is not used literally according to linguistic laws and usage. In Jewish worship, the context of Christ's worship and early Christian worship (cf. Matt. 5:17), the worshiper participated by association in the sacrifice.[7] The word "body" is used partly because it is a correlative of the word "blood," and partly because it is a correlative to "spirit." To give the body for someone naturally means to die, to give one's soul. But the term "body" instead of "the soul" is used because He is instituting the symbolic means of the Eucharist, which is not the symbolic eating of the flesh of Christ, but His sacrificial act. The meaning of the text is derived from His sacrificial, bodily death (Luke 23:46).

At the Last Supper Jesus, as leader, performed the break-

[6] Cf. Higgins, J. B., *The Lord's Supper in the New Testament,* (London: SCM, 1960), p. 50.

[7] Cf. Taylor, Vincent, *Jesus and His Sacrifice,* (London: Macmillan & Company, 1951), p. 121.

ing of bread, and realizing His approaching death His soul stirred within Him. How very natural then was it for Him to act and say when He was performing the service of breaking bread: "This is just what will happen to me at my death." But "the dying itself was not as important to him as the purpose of his sacrificial death."[8] It is not difficult to understand why Jesus should choose the bread as the symbol of His body, and the breaking of it as the breaking of His body, for it was a common and likely symbol. This choice of Jesus gives clear indication that He never did, and does not now, intend the symbol in any way to be associated with "flesh." The concept of "bread and life" prevails throughout the life and teaching of the Lord (Matt. 4:3, 4; 7:9; 15:33; 16:11; Mark 6:36, 37; 8:4; Luke 11:3; 14:15; John 6:31ff.).

The relation of "this" to "my body" is defined by the copula "is," Greek *estic*. In Jesus' language, Aramaic, the inference is "means," "represents," or "stands for." The hard literal English translation "is," is not characteristic of the language. The translation of "is" can be interpreted spiritually, and is nearer the truth than a "natural" interpretation. This is the point that has caused deep division in the Church.

The "is" should not be made to imply an actual identity. There can be no question of identity here any more than in such expressions as "I am the door." "I am the way." "I am the vine," or "the rock of Christ" (John 10:7; 14:6; 15:1; I Cor. 10:4). At the time most of these statements were spoken, Jesus was still present in the flesh, which obviously excluded any confusion or any idea of one substance being changed into another.[9]

On the other hand, "is" must not simply be understood in the sense of "signifies." In our English language this would greatly weaken the close connection Christ made between Himself and the symbol of the bread. The interpretation,

[8] Dalman, Gustof, *Jesus-Jesha,* (London: S.P.C.K., 1929), p. 144.

[9] Ramseyer, J. P., "Lord's Supper," in *A Companion to the Bible,* (New York: Oxford University Press, 1958), p. 241.

"This means my body," is probably nearest the truth and teaches us that the bread is a divine symbol with spiritual mystery.

In any case the truth of this eucharistic saying is to be found, not in "is," but in "*Take ye, this* is *my body*." The significance of the paschal lamb is what it represented, the efficacious death of the lambs in Egypt. In the same way the bread and wine of the Eucharist represent the atoning sacrifice of Christ as the true paschal lamb without possessing any inherent efficacy. The Last Supper was the point of the institution of the Eucharist. What is to be emphasized is not the eucharistic elements themselves, but the sacrificial act they call to mind.[10]

The significance of the total saying within Holy Communion and Christian worship is supreme. These genuine words of the Lord clearly define His passion, not as a martyrdom, but as a sacrifice for man. He was the singular figure in the event of the Cross; yet it was meant for the experience of all mankind, to be appropriated by man. Jesus instituted the sacrament of "breaking bread" whereby we can fellowship in His sufferings and share in His resurrected life.

The eucharistic element of the bread is made sacramental by promise and by use; it is never transmuted into substance. It is changed with Christ but not converted into Christ, as the spoken words are changed with the Gospel but are not themselves the Gospel. As the Church does not prolong Christ's incarnation but confers and conveys it, so the bread in the Eucharist does not continue the body of Christ, but mediates it, by the Holy Spirit through faith.

THE SAYING OVER THE CUP. There are many forms of criticism surrounding these sayings. The idea of blood is thought to be entirely repulsive to any Jew, including Jesus and His disciples. Mark's "cup saying" does not follow the

[10] Cf. Higgins, *op. cit.,* p. 93.

same formula as the "bread saying" and is therefore regarded by some as a later appendage to Scripture. However, it should be noted that Mark's Gospel is short, rough, and unpolished in style. Mark's Gospel is a collection of some of the sayings and dynamic actions of the Lord, loosely hung together like a string of pearls with a rough knot between them. In such a style there is no need for the "cup saying" to be exactly like the "bread saying." We believe that the saying recorded in Mark is original, from the Last Supper of the Lord.[11] Concerning the objection of the "blood symbol" in Jewish and human thought, Vincent Taylor says, "I think it is a fair rejoinder to this argument to say, first, that it is not a question of what a Palestinian or Galilean Jew would be likely to suggest, but of what might be commanded by a Jew who believed himself to be the Son of man destined to suffer on behalf of many."[12] In the sense of "human niceness" Jesus did not presume to bring peace but a sword (Matt. 10:34). His teaching was considered hard (John 6:31-58), and even His own family thought He was beside Himself (Mark 3:21).

The similarity of the passages in Mark and I Corinthians 11 causes some to raise the question whether one was a copy of the other. However, the basic concepts of the two passages are distinguishable. The passage in Mark, "blood of the covenant," is based on Exodus 24:8 and Isaiah 53:12. The Pauline passage, "new covenant," rests on a combination of Jeremiah 31:41 and the concepts of Exodus 24:1-13. We can quickly answer this proposed question by pointing out that they are similar enough to show they are authentic, and yet enough different to demonstrate their originality.

The only one who could have used these words, "This is my blood of the new covenant which is poured out for many," with sacred meaning and holy relevancy was Jesus Christ, Son of God – and He did.

[11] Cf. Taylor, *op. cit.*, pp. 133-134.
[12] *Ibid.*

The meaning of the saying cannot fully be realized in human language. Words become finite in declaring this infinite truth. However, we understand the background of the saying in the institution of the Law. The account of the institution of the Old Covenant in Exodus 24 relates Moses coming to the people with the words of God. In hearing the word of God the people declare their pledge to God. An altar is built for the sacrificial offering, following the reading of the covenant with God, to bring blessings of God to them. The sprinkling of the altar is the symbol of God's sealing the covenant with His people.

The Old Testament worship of sacrificial offering and sprinkling of blood is a symbolic means of sealing the covenant between God and man. It was a temporary type repeated over and over (cf. Heb. 10, 11). The sacrificial offering of Jesus Christ is the permanent antitype which is never repeated, for which the "cup of blessing" is the spiritual symbol in the Eucharist. The Lord distinctly pointed out the reason why His blood will have significance for others: it is the seal of the New Covenant (settlement). According to Matthew and Mark it is "My blood of the covenant"; according to Paul it is the cup which is "the new covenant in my blood." The concept of "covenant" always suggests the joining together of several parties, and it is an axiom that a later covenant abrogates a former.[13] Jesus with one stroke boldly removed the foundation of the Passover feast and the whole Old Testament dispensation, and replaced it with something new, the Eucharist of Christian Holy Communion.

The use of wine as a symbol of blood is not new in the Old Testament (Gen. 49:11; Deut. 34:14; Isa. 63:36; Eccles. 39:26). This prevailing concept prepared the way for the institution of the cup as a sacramental symbol in Holy Communion. How very natural then for Jesus to use the cup of blessing at the Last Supper as a symbol of His shed blood

[13] Dalman, *op. cit.*, p. 162.

in the institution of the Eucharist. Jesus was also familiar with the significance of the cup in the Prophets and the Psalms, that it was a symbol of a bitter destiny, and that one was ordained to empty the cup with all its bitter contents (Isa. 51:17; Jer. 25:5; Ezek. 23:23; Ps. 11:6; 60:5; 75:9). Our Lord often used this simile in His later ministry, applying it to His approaching sacrificial death (Matt. 20:22; 26: 39, 42; John 18:11).

The cup which Jesus took to bless and institute in the Last Supper was most probably the cup of blessing following the main meal. This interpretation fits the accounts of Matthew and Mark, also the Pauline account of the cup which the Lord took after the meal (I Cor. 11:25), and the saying "cup of blessing" (I Cor. 10:16). The prayer of blessing at the Last Supper had the striking new words of Jesus who symbolically transferred its essential meaning to Himself as the Suffering Savior. "This is my blood" thus means, this wine which I give you is like unto my blood which shall flow for your benefit. It is also significant that He chose the cup of "blessing" to declare eternally the meaning of the shedding of His blood! Jesus Christ is not the martyr of the Jews, but the Son of God who laid down His life. The Scriptural accounts specify that *all* the disciples drank *all* of the cup. The distribution was complete and the cup was completely emptied. The participation of the disciples, as of all disciples, in the life of the Lord was to be complete, in His sufferings and in His blessings. Jesus desired the complete communion of the disciples with Himself: "Drink ye all of it." According to Israelitish belief, the blood is conceived of as being apart from the body and stands for the outpoured life. When this life blood is shed, the soul with the blood as its seat leaves the body with it (Gen. 9:4; Lev. 17:14; Deut. 12: 23). The Israelites avoided a magical concept of the Passover blood by emphasizing that it was not the *blood* per se that God recognized, but the manifestation of Himself in the covenant. So we as Christians in the New Covenant partake of the "inner spring always welling up for eternal life" (John 4:15).

The phrase of the passage, "which is poured out for many" signifies a violent death, in behalf of others. This is the vicarious action of a sinless Christ for sinful men. The "pouring out" is the deliberate action of the sacrificing one, Jesus Christ our High Priest, who laid down His life and "poured out" His blood in completely vicarious action. "The many," in the narrow sense, is the house of Israel; in the broad sense it is the whole world who will enter into His "settlement of sin." Christ is alone in the sacrificial act of the Cross, but His vicarious atonement is for "the many" To the world it appeared that He was left alone, but precisely at this point the "many" were wrought into the Kingdom of God (cf. Eph. 1:7-10).

The words, "for the forgiveness of sins," are the New Covenant of forgiveness, spoken of by the prophet Jeremiah (Jer. 31:34). The means of this forgiveness through the "Suffering Servant" are revealed by the prophet Isaiah (Isa. 53). Forgiveness of sins is the prerogative of God (Matt. 9:5, 6), participated in by man. This is the eternal purpose of God in His Son, Jesus Christ. The Servant of God in Isaiah 53 bears in His sufferings the punishment for the sins of others, for it is impossible for sinful man to bear his own sins before God, and the righteousness and justice of God demand that sin shall not remain unpunished.

The eucharistic text, "This is my blood of the New Covenant which is poured out for many for the remission of sins," is ultimately the love of God. For God so loved that He gave His Son, that all men might know He is just and the justifier of all who have faith in Christ. Love is the basis of God's action and man's redeemed salvation, supremely symbolized in the "cup of blessing" of the Eucharist.

THE COMMAND TO REPEAT. From the very beginning of the infant Church the remembrance of the sacrificial act of Jesus Christ was considered obligatory (Acts 2:42). From the record in Acts it cannot be doubted that the disciples wanted to be united with the risen Lord in the breaking of bread and the drinking of the cup. From His breaking bread at the Last Supper the disciples continued in the ever-new breaking of bread of the Eucharist of Holy Communion. The remembrances of the cup and of the bread are, according to the Pauline account, independent of one another. The order of the Last Supper separated the bread and the cup: breaking bread, main meal, and cup of blessing. This distinctive action of the bread and cup is now integrated into the Eucharist of the Holy Communion.

The early Gospel of Mark does not include the saying of "remembrance," which is included in the Pauline text and in the later Gospel of Luke. The omission in Mark does not invalidate the saying in any way, because he was not discribing the "Eucharist" as such, but the occurrences of the Last Supper. Mark succinctly records the sayings which give meaning to what the Church was already remembering in practice.

St. Paul is the first, in point of time, to account for the commanding words, "This do in remembrance of me." The suggestion that Paul could have invented the words as recorded in I Cor. 11:15 is incredible. The responsibility for the historical truth of I Cor. 11 concerning the Last Supper rests not on Paul, but on the Jerusalem Church, and ultimately on Peter, James, and the other disciples who were present at the Last Supper. I Cor. 11 describes the practice of the Eucharist in the infant Church within ten years of the time of the Last Supper. The account in Mark 14 expresses the same eucharistic practice in the form which it had reached when Mark wrote. That these accounts are accurate is evidenced by the strong tradition of the Apostles, also by the fact that the different "parties," such as the Judaizers, were constantly observing Paul's ministry. They would have brought charges against him if he had taught or practiced the Eucharist in a way different from the Apostolic tradition. It is interesting to note in passing that this is one of two traditions within the life of the early Church which are so vital to the faith that Paul does not trust his own terms, but repeats the evidence in the verbal form in which he had received it (cf. I Cor. 11:23; 15:1-3).

The Greek word *anamnesis*, "remembrance," is not as easily translated into English as it might appear. For in English "remembrance," or memorial, has the connotation of something completely past and absent which is mentally recollected. However, both the Old and New Testament Scriptures give the sense of the word as "re-calling" or "representing" before God an event in the past so that it becomes here and now operative by its effects. This connotation takes the word out of the concept of "sentimental memory." However, it does not place it in the other extreme position of an actual re-sacrificing.[14] Old Testament examples of "remembrance" are found in Leviticus 24:7, "That it may be on the bread for a memorial"; and Numbers 10:10, the blowing of the trumpets "shall be a memorial for you before your God." Since there are other Biblical words for "sacrificial offering" and since there is not sufficient evidence to assert that "remembrance" is an act of sacrificial offering, we reject this sense in the Eucharist. The sense of the word can best be described as neither a "sentimental" nor a "sacrificial" memorial, but a spiritual, symbolic memorial wrought by the Holy Spirit .

The concept of remembrance was most certainly in the sphere of the Passover week. At the eating of the unleavened bread the exodus from Egypt was to be remembered (Exod. 13:3, 9; Deut. 16:3), and the paschal offering itself was meant to be a remembrance (Exod. 12:14). The paschal lamb was related to these teachings in that it was to be remembered that God had passed over the houses of the Israelities in Egypt,

[14] The position of the Roman Catholic Church.

and the blood at the door-posts should be a remembrance for all time (Exod. 12:4). The re-telling of this ancient story of Israel was to be so vivid that each new generation thought itself actually present at that Egyptian Passover. Therefore, the Lord's teaching concerning "remembrance" at the Last Supper is perceived and practiced by the disciples in the early Church.

The remembrance of the Lord is instituted by Christ for mankind that tends quickly to forget. The central thought is not the glib human request, "Do not forget me," or the desire to continue the Palestinian personal relationship between the Lord and His disciples. The deep sense is that on the "Easter side" of the Cross men need to recall His sacrificial act, appropriate the atonement of God provided by the Cross, and to claim Him as their Lord and Master.

THE ESCHATOLOGICAL NATURE IN THE EUCHARISTIC SAYINGS. Jesus' vow-promise, "I shall not drink again . . . until that day when I drink it new in the Kingdom of God," is probably derived from three types of religious vows.[15] One vow is that of common renunciation sealed with a religious promise (cf. Num. 30:2-17; I Sam. 14:14, 24; Ps. 132:2-5). A second type is the Nazarite vow by which the individual forgoes natural practices in complete dedication to a cause (cf. Luke 2:37; I Cor. 7:15). Probably John the Baptist forwent meat and drink for the heralding of the coming Christ (Luke 7:33). A third type of vow is significant in Judaism, for it is a resolution in prayer (cf. I Sam. 14:24; II Sam. 12:15ff.; Ps. 109:24). An example of a prayer-vow is, "For thou, O God, hast heard my vows" (Ps. 61:6). This concept of prayer-vow is probably in the background of Jesus' vow, "I shall not drink again. . ." Jesus has resolutely set Himself for this shadow of the Cross, for the shedding of His blood. Jesus affirms to Himself and to

[15] Cf. Jeremias, *op. cit.*, pp. 165-172.

His disciples that the will of God in the "suffering servant" is irrevocable. The dreadful soul struggle depicted in Gethsemane has already begun in the upper room. The pitting of the forces of Satan against God, which began in the wilderness temptations, has never ceased and is now approaching the final hour. The "Body" (cf. Heb. 10:5) that was prepared for the incarnation of the Son of God is brought near the "valley of death" bearing the sin of the world, with the prayer-vow of complete fulfillment.

The saying in Mark, "drink again," indicates that Jesus did drink the "cup of blessing" with His disciples. And while the disciples' attention was naturally present, Jesus' attention was naturally future. The disciples were looking toward His suffering; Jesus was anticipating the resurrection. "If death is certain, so is reunion."[16] Jesus' prayer-vow is an irrevocable resolution; "nevertheless not what I will, but what thou wilt" (Mark 14:36).

The "newness" spoken of in the vow is a "new kind," rather than a new supply of the same old kind. The time has come when the offering of dumb bulls and goats shall stop, when the celebration of the Passover shall cease, and God will inaugurate the eternal Passover. The next meal, perhaps in the same upper room, which Jesus will hold with His disciples will be a new Messianic meal, on an earth that has experienced a resurrection. And this seals the promise of the consummation when there shall be a "new heaven and a new earth, for the former things are passed away, and he that sat upon the throne said, Behold, I make all things new" (Rev. 21:1-5).

The concept of the Kingdom of God in the eucharistic sayings, is also evident in the teachings of the Lord from the beginning to the end of His ministry (cf. Matt. 4:17). Jesus did not replace or change His earlier teaching, for He always taught with authority. There is no conflict in the concept

[16] Taylor, *op. cit.*, p. 141.

of the Kingdom of God and the Christ event. On the contrary, the Kingdom of God is established by His giving Himself on the Cross. Christ is so certain of the establishment of the Kingdom of God, even at the Last Supper, that He assures His disciples that He will not drink the cup of blessing again "until that day when I drink it new in the Kingdom of God." Jesus' saying is not a despairing hope, but a prayer-vow of resolution. This saying is not a hidden parable, but the public proclamation of the eternal purpose of God in Christ.

We turn now to some of the main Christian teachings based upon the eucharistic sayings of the Lord.

The Spiritual Presence of Christ in the Eucharist

Christ is eternally present in the cosmos, everlastingly present in the Church, continually present in the Christian, and supremely present in the Eucharist of Holy Communion. The ineffable mystery of the Eucharist is that in it God, who is eternally with Himself, continues through the Church in the world, yet independent of it. We pause to reflect that in this infinite mystery of the presence of Christ in us which transcends our comprehension, we come more to adore than to discuss. The mystery of the presence of Christ in the Eucharist is like unto the mystery of God incarnate in the Babe of Bethlehem, unto whom the wise men came, bowed down, and worshiped. In the Eucharist there is an identity of man in God, "For while we remain in Him, and He remains in the Father, and remaining in the Father remains in us, thus advancing us to unity with the Father."[17] This identity with God through Christ becomes more real to us in the celebration of the Eucharist.

The consideration of the presence of Christ in the Eucharist is not *whether* He is present at the Holy Communion, but *how* He is present. There is little doubt that the Holy Com-

[17] Torrance, T. F., *Conflict and Agreement In the Church,* (London: Lutterworth Press, 1960), p. 144.

munion revolves around Christ's words, "This is my body broken for you. . . This is my blood shed for you." Yet these very plain words have raised many questions in the Church. Are the bread and cup literally or spiritually the body and blood of Christ? Is the presence of Christ spatial or spiritual? Is the presence objective or subjective? Is it in substance or symbol – or a combination of them? Of course, we do not believe or teach from the Holy Scriptures that the body and blood of Christ are naturally present in the elements of the Eucharist; yet Christ is spiritually present. Our faith must avoid all the magical, mechanical and spatial implications of saying that the body and blood are *in* the bread and the cup. No prayer of consecration has power to change the elements of the Eucharist into the substance of the body and blood of Christ. Our faith must also avoid the opposite error of assuming to make the presence of Christ dependent upon the superficial, subjective mood and human emotion of the communicant. Neither the priestly prayer of consecration, nor the mere faith of the communicant makes God present in the Eucharist. God is present in the Eucharist in and through Himself. Surely our genuine Christian faith must gladly affirm the truth that Christ is spiritually present in the bread and cup of Holy Communion.

Belief in *how* Christ is present in the Holy Communion, however, divides the Church. The crass doctrine of transubstantiation of the Roman Latin Church was a concept that evolved with the mind of the dark Middle Age in wanting to "see" rather than to exercise faith. The Roman Latin doctrine was first systematically presented in the writings of Paschasius Radbertus, "On the Body and Blood of the Lord," in A.D. 844. This work asserts that the bread and wine are changed by consecration into the body and blood of Christ that were *born of Mary*.[18] It remained for Thomas Aquinas to define

[18] Fortescue, Adrian, "Mass", *The Catholic Encyclopedia,* (New York: The Appleton Company, 1910), Vol. IX, pp. 790ff.

the doctrine. In writing about the presence of Christ in the Eucharist, he states that it is not local, but is after the manner of a substance, and that the whole Christ, body and blood, is present in each particle of the sacrament and under each species by concomitance.[19] The extreme position of the doctrine was stated by Pius IV in the Council of Trent, "I profess that in the Mass is offered to God a pure, proper and propitiatory sacrifice, . . . and that there does take place a conversion of the entire substance of the bread into the body, and of the entire substance of the wine into the blood, which conversion the Catholic Church doth call Transubstantiation."[20]

In the ensuing centuries this doctrine has been a deep source of embarrassment to the Roman Church, and until this day it is seeking to remove this basic error from its doctrine. The crude Roman Catholic concept of priesthood, which repeats the sacrifice of Christ in a propitiatory sense, assuming to control man's eternal life, with sacerdotal control over the body of Christ, is untenable with the Gospel of Jesus Christ. The Roman concept of a priest being the bridge between man and God by re-enacting the sacrifice of Christ in the Mass is contrary to the whole life and Person of Christ. Christ said, "I am the way . . . no one comes to the Father except by me" (John 14:6).

The Reformers violently reacted to the Roman "Mass-Eucharist" in many ways. Luther declared the doctrine of the real presence of Christ's body and blood in the Eucharist, together with (consubstantiation) the bread and wine. Zwingli asserted that the Eucharist was an act of commemoration, a visible sign of His body and blood. Calvin interpreted that in the Eucharist the consecrated elements bear an essential relation to the substance.

In rejecting the eucharistic teachings of others, we must

[19] Cf. Thomas Aquinas, *Summa Theology III,* 71.1.6.

[20] Torry, D. F., "Mass," *The Encyclopedia Britannica,* (London: Cambridge University Press), 1911 edition, Vol. 17, p. 849.

have a real teaching of our own concerning the presence of Christ in the Eucharist. First of all, when we speak of the presence of Christ in the Eucharist, we understand that this is but one manifestation of Christ's presence. Christ said, "For where two or three have met together in my name, I am there among them" (Matt. 18:20). This means that Christ is present in the corporate body of the Church. Christ is also present in the individual Christian. In the very night of passion Christ prayed in His high priestly prayer, "I in them. . ." (John 17:23). Paul declared, "I have been crucified with Christ; the life I now live is not my life, but the life which Christ lives *in me*. . ." (Gal. 2:20). "Christ may dwell in your hearts through faith" was the prayer of Paul for the Ephesians (Eph. 3:17).

Christ is also omnipresent, everywhere present. However, when we say that Christ is omnipresent, it is understood that He is not in every atom; this would be pantheism. In fact, God is not in matter or space, for matter and space are a part of His creation, and He Himself transcends it. The Christian doctrine of omnipresence means that wherever we are in this life and world of time and matter and space, we are not apart from God, and He is not absent from us.

The presence of Christ in the Eucharist is a special presence. There are times in life when realities become "more real." Certainly, in hours of worship, reading the Holy Scriptures, and prayer God is present in a way that He is not present in the kitchen, field, or factory. The place does not determine the reality of the person of God, but the realization of the presence of God. In this sense the Pedilavium and the Agape are significantly important in that they prepare the believer for the realization of the spiritual presence of Christ in the Eucharist.

The presence of Christ in the Eucharist is spiritual not simply because He can't be seen. If we were totally spiritual we might not see Him. He is spiritually present because of the spiritual purpose to which the bread and cup are used by the

Holy Spirit. In the New Testament sense, being spiritual is more than "sightlessness," or being opposite to the material. For instance, a person may not be "materialistically minded" and still not be "spiritually minded." In the New Testament sense of the term, a thing or person is spiritual only when the Holy Spirit is effectively manifest and in effective control. Isaac was born "after the Spirit" in contrast to Ishmael, who was born "after the flesh," not because he was less materially born, but because the Holy Spirit was specially evident in the circumstances of his birth. Thus the spiritual presence of Christ in the Eucharist is in the fact that the divine Spirit is supremely manifest in the bread and cup, and supremely effective in the communicant.

The spiritual presence of Christ does not make the presence less real. The presence of Christ in the Eucharist is real; real, first of all, in the sense of genuine presence. Every Christian, regardless of eucharistic doctrine, must believe that Christ's presence is genuine. Christ's sayings, "This is my body . . . This is my blood" preclude any belief other than that the genuineness of Christ's presence of "Himself" in the Eucharist does not mean His physical sense, His resurrected sense, or His glorified sense, but His sense as in the Holy Spirit of the Trinity. It is important to realize that Christ Himself, the "whole Christ," is present in the Eucharist in order to avoid a superficial belief of His presence as an ethical quality or a spiritual influence. The "totus Christus" is present in the Eucharist as He was in the incarnation, the Cross, the resurrection, and the ascension. The imperative point to maintain is the distinction between the true reality of Christ spiritually present in the Eucharist and the physical elements themselves. The bread and wine are instruments of His will which He can at pleasure use or discard; and to which He is in no subtlest way subjective.[21] "God sanctifies and uses material things as

[21] Gore, *op. cit.,* 132.

channels of the Holy Spirit, but He does not deify them."[22] The truth of God comes to us in "clay earthly vessels," and earthen vessels are sanctified through that of which they are the vehicle, but the vessel is never equated with the contents.

The doctrine of the Eucharist must harmonize with all other Christian teaching. Christian doctrine must always interrelate and harmonize. It is a matter of Church history that many doctrines have been misleading and in error because they are not harmonized with the total Christ and the entire Gospel. The teaching of the atonement has often been untrue to the Gospel because it was not based on the foundation of one God in three persons, and on the fact that the persons of the Trinity are one in love and will. The humanity of Christ is often stressed to the exclusion of the deity of Christ, as illustrated in the Jesus of History and Christ of Faith controversy. These illustrations press upon us the importance of interpreting the Eucharist in the context of the total Gospel. One of the doctrines of the Gospel to which the teachings of the Eucharist must be closely related is the doctrine of the Holy Spirit. God's every act, His love and mercy, come through the Person of the Holy Spirit; therefore, the divine action and grace that come in the Eucharist come through the Holy Spirit. The order of God's coming to man, His revelation, was Father-Son-Holy Spirit. Therefore, the order of man's going to God is the converse: Holy Spirit-Son-Father. This is the New Testament order, and it must not, and can not be changed. Therefore, in the "church age" the "realness" of God shall be had only through the Holy Spirit and through the ordained means the Holy Spirit chooses to use, such as the bread and cup. Christ is spiritually present in the Eucharist through His person of the Holy Spirit.

Christian worship is essentially a worship in spirit and in truth. "God is spirit, and those who worship him must wor-

[22] Paul, Robert S., *The Atonement and the Sacraments,* (London: Hodder and Stoughton, 1961), p. 373.

ship in spirit and in truth" (John 4:24). In spirit because all believers have immediate access to God through the Son; in truth, because the Son has perfectly revealed the Father. The relevance of this basic Christian truth to the Eucharist is not in the meaning of the symbols per se, but in their place in the whole Gospel.

If we would presume to limit God's grace to the sacrament of Holy Communion alone, we would be presuming to limit God, and this is nonsense. On the other hand, when we understand the perpetual presence of Christ in the members of the Church, we understand the Eucharist as a climaxing part, not an exclusive or concluding part in Holy Communion. To understand this is to worship God "in spirit and truth." In a word – *Christ through the Holy Spirit is not just a visitor in the Christian's heart; He is an abiding guest, sometimes in special "garments" of celebration.*

The real spiritual presence of Christ in the Eucharist is also personal. The book, *The Theology of the Sacraments*, by D. M. Baillie, illustrates this truth by pointing out that a chair may be *alongside* a table and beside the table, but not really *with* the table in the true sense. Likewise, there may be two persons together in a room, without their being in more than a space relationship with each other; they have not established a genuine relationship. We can have someone who is sitting next to us, someone whom we can look at and listen to and whom we can touch if we want to – and yet is farther from us than some *loved one* who is perhaps thousands of miles away, or perhaps, no longer among the living.[23]

There is nothing more real than what comes in Christian faith. "The man who demands a reality more solid than that of the Christian consciousness knows not what he seeks."[24] The abiding spiritual presence of Christ in the cosmos, the Church

[23] Baillie, *op. cit.*, p. 99.

[24] Wotherspoon, H. J., *Religious Values In the Sacraments,* (Edinburgh: T. & T. Clark, 1928), p. 104.

and the Christian, reaches a certain climax in the Eucharist of Holy Communion. Here God, who was incarnate in Jesus, uses an ordained sacramental symbol as a special means of stirring the faith of His people that they may receive Him, since faith is the channel by which the Father's most real presence comes to men in this life.

The Communicant's Faith in the Eucharist

In the previous section we concluded that the presence of Christ in the bread and cup is spiritually real, *through faith.* Now the means whereby the spiritual conjunction between God and man in the Eucharist takes place must be discerned. How does God come to us and how do we receive Christ in our hearts? What is the means employed by God, and the means man employs, God's action and man's reaction? God's action in the Eucharist is through His *Holy Spirit* who offers us Himself in spiritual conjunction. Man's means in receiving this action of God is *faith.* There must be faith in man's heart to receive the bread and cup of God. Therefore, the Holy Spirit and faith are the two means employed in this spiritual conjunction.

The presence of God received by faith is the most real presence possible in this world. The reality perceived through faith is penetrating and abiding, in contrast to reality through sight that is very limited and fleeting. "Sight" reality is limited by the nearest obstacle. We can't see around a tree, beyond the horizon, or through to the heart of man. The sense of sight is as fleeting as the blink of the eye and usually the first sense of the human being to weaken and "wear out." Faith reality, on the other hand, as a means of perceiving, has no material limitation and is as eternal as the soul.

Faith as the means of receiving Christ in the Eucharist was lost in the Church of the Medieval Age because it had lost the Word of God. The Word of God was not taught or preached in the vernacular of the people whereby they could have the means of faith to perceive Christ in the Eucharist. Because of this lack of faith the people were insistent on *seeing* the action of the Eucharist. This demand of the people who were untaught in Holy Scripture and lacked the means of faith resulted in the doctrine of relating the elements of the Eucharist to the substance of the body and blood of Christ. The Roman Catholics went along with this common crassness of the people in wanting to "see" Christ in the Eucharist. The Roman Latins never quite said you could "see" Christ in the Eucharist, but neither did they condemn this common trend. The Reformers corrected this error by teaching the Word of God in the language of the people and bringing faith to the hearts of Christians whereby they could perceive Christ in the Eucharist by faith. From this background we can easily understand why the Reformers put such great emphasis on the Holy Scriptures and kept the Eucharist closely related to it: "Faith cometh by hearing, and hearing by the word of God" (Rom. 10:17).

The Church Fathers used ambiguous language in describing the individual's subjective faith and the objective reality of Christ in the Eucharist. Augustine's famous statement, "Believe and thou hast eaten,"[25] is an example. However, the early Church always held the concept of faith as basic to the plain language concerning the body and blood in the bread and cup.

The emphasis upon faith in the Eucharist is criticised as being too subjective, too human, in contrast to the objective once-and-for-all sacrificial act of Christ symbolized in the Communion. This is not a valid criticism for two primary reasons. First of all, in the broad sense, the means of faith in the Eucharist is not just an independent faith based upon the precarious state of mind of an individual. There is the existence of the common faith held by the total Church in the "totus Christus." The Church is the body of Christ and

[25] Augustine, *In John* 25:12.

is the ordained preserver of the faith in Him. It is in this common faith that all communicants share by degree. This common faith held by the Church is somewhat like common reason in the natural world whereby objective truth can be verified. Therefore, the truth of Christ in the Eucharist through the means of faith is not based on the precarious nature of man, but is related to the total faith of the Church, which in turn is based on the abiding presence of the Holy Spirit.

The fact of the common faith held by the Church answers the question concerning those communicants coming to the Eucharist with little or no faith. "For while Communion gets its value from faith, it does not depend on the immediate faith of individual communicants, nor on their number."[26] Communion is the act of the Church as well as the act of the individual, and the Church does all that Christ means to do through the sacrament, even if there are individuals present without faith, that is, if it is a living Church of the New Creation and observes His commands in faith and obedience. The Lord's Supper is essentially a communal act, the supreme worship center of the family of God.

Secondly, the essence of faith in the Eucharist is not a psychological or intellectual thing. Faith in essence is not a rational acceptance of certain historical facts and principles of truths which would place the meaning of the Eucharist in the hands of man rather than God. Faith is not an emotional state stirred up by designed factors. Faith itself is a gift of God. Faith is the total response of man, which arises from the belief that Christ died for our sins. Faith comes as a new being in man through the Holy Spirit. It is a fact of being begotten by the Holy Spirit, which is in contrast to a piece of knowledge or an opinion or a flight of fancy. Faith constitutes a new relation between man and God, in which

[26] Forsyth, P. T., *The Church and the Sacraments,* (London: Longmans, Green, 1917), p. 258.

the deepest anxiety is overcome, and in which Christ dwells in our souls, "Faith is our moral response to the cross, not our qualification."[27] This is the essence of the faith that the Reformers used in interpreting the Eucharist and the Gospel.[28] This is the essence of the faith that we use today in appropriating the Eucharist. The faith that we use in the Eucharist is not based upon a mental or emotional nature, but on our new nature created in us through the Holy Spirit. Our faith is not based upon a human category, but a divine creation. This God-given faith in our spirits by the Holy Spirit frees us from any idea of natural substance in the Eucharist and makes real the act of God in Jesus Christ on the cross.

His dwelling in our hearts by faith, "That Christ may dwell in your hearts by faith" (Eph. 3:17), is *identified* by faith but not identical with *faith*. Through faith we partake of the bread and cup, and through this same faith, not the bread and cup, Christ communes with us. The significance of the eucharistic communion is in the fact that by the eternal Holy Spirit the Christian by faith, together with the believing Church, is given to step over the natural boundary and partake of the divine nature.

The means of faith in the Eucharist must be held within the context of the whole Christian faith. The resurrected Christ has ascended to the right hand of God and is now not replaced, nor made identical, but present through the Holy Spirit. The Son and Spirit work in the unity of the Trinity, whether in historical objectivity or subjectivity, whether at Bethlehem or Pentecost, or between Pentecost and the *parousia*.[29] The presence of God in His Holy Spirit today is invisible, perceived only by invisible faith. The worship of God through the Holy Communion can never be realized by the sense of sight, but by the sense of faith. Christ through the Holy

[27] Forsyth, *op. cit.,* p. 217.
[28] Cf. Richardson, C. G., *Zwingli and Cranmer on the Eucharist,* (Evanston: Illinois, Seabury Seminary, 1949), p. 6.
[29] Clark, *op. cit.,* p. 76.

Spirit is invisible, veiled in His Word and sacraments. This veiling of Christ in the Eucharist is called a "mystery." It is a mystery, not as the unknown, certainly not in the sense of magic, but as unseen. The mystery of Christ is now made known to our hearts by the Holy Spirit (cf. Rom. 8), and the veil of sight shall be removed only at the time of *parousia* when we shall "see Him face to face" (I Cor. 13:12).

As earthen beings in an earthen world let us be content with earthen symbols of the bread and cup. May we accept this earthen vessel as used by the Holy Spirit to bring a reaffirmation of Christ to the Church, and the "real presence" of Christ to our hearts. The bread and cup are appropriate symbols of the presently veiled Christ. The ordained bread and cup in Holy Communion give us more than mere words which are slowly heard and quickly forgotten. The Eucharist is indeed realizing the spiritual presence of Christ by the Holy Spirit through faith. "Faith gives substance to our hopes, and makes us certain of realities we do not see" (Heb. 11:1).

In the Holy Communion God says to us, Take Christ's vicarious death in your life through faith. The sinner comes by faith to the Cross, and the eternal life through the Cross comes to him. The sinner is united with the crucified and risen Savior through faith. By faith we receive His gift of life, and He takes upon Himself what is rightfully our sentence of death. This substitution, through the means of the Holy Spirit and faith, is the grace of God in Jesus Christ.

The "Remembrance" of the Eucharist

The eucharistic passage includes the words, "This do in remembrance of me." In what way does the Church "remember" the one who is *alive*, who *is* our very life, and still *present* and acting with us? Discard immediately any inclination to believe that Christ's command to repeat is a mere memorial. There is nothing which subtracts more from Holy Communion than to go through it as an act of mere commemoration. The Reformers all insisted that it was more than historical faith.[30] "Remembering" is not for us a sentimental reverie, thinking how we would love to have been with Him there. The Eucharist of Holy Communion is the sacramental symbol of the Cross, not the act of the Cross itself, but the transfer of it to the believer. As Dean Forsyth described it, "The word is repeated often, but the thought is there once for all. In music we repeat the performance often by means of the score (the elements); but the composer's finished work stands there, ideally, eternally functioning in many generations. So Christ's redeeming act functioning in the Supper, conveying itself to its beneficiaries, and it goes on doing so in the Church."[31] In the repeating of the Eucharist, Christ is repeatedly conveyed to us in this special way. The act of Christ on the Cross is done and received of the Father once and forever; it cannot ever be repeated, but it can be and is given to us anew.

The early Church was quick to realize that it was between Christ's incarnation and Christ's consummation. The disciples were filled with the memories of Christ, the Cross, the resurrection, and the ascension. They were also filled, almost to the point of explosion, with the promises of Christ concerning His coming again to consummate the Gospel. The whole concept of "in remembrance of me," is in itself historical. Each Communion service was a dramatization of the past; the Supper, Golgotha, and Easter Day, with the burning belief of the coming "crowning day." It is significantly true that in Christianity the historical reference to the act of Christ, the Christ event, determined the heart of Communion, "Do this in remembrance of *me*." In this interim period, of memory of the past and hope of the future,[32] the Eucharist

[30] Cf. Richardson, *op. cit.,* p. 11.
[31] Forsyth, *op. cit.,* p. 223.
[32] Cf. Baillie, *op. cit.,* p. 102.

became the dramatic symbol in Christian worship. The paradox of the faith became evident in this period in the sense of Christ's "presence in absence." Paul affirmed that "Christ lives in me," and at the same time, "we are absent from the Lord" (Gal. 2:20; II Cor. 5:6). They no more knew Christ after the flesh; nevertheless His presence was more real than when they walked beside Him in Jerusalem or Capernaum. From this same interim position of looking back to the Cross of Christ and forward to the consummation of Christ, we can understand the command of Christ to repeat the Lord's Supper "in remembrance of me."

The Eucharist is a genuine memorial feast of the passion of the Lord. Its historical foundation in the Christ of the Cross at the crux of history is what clearly distinguishes the Lord's Supper from religious cultism. In Christianity the essence is the communicant's response of faith to the Christ event. In pagan religions the worshiper pleads for the acceptance of his own natural offering. In Christian worship we praise God for the offering of His Son, Jesus Christ.

The Lord's Supper is a memorial like the altar set up by Jacob at Bethel and the twelve stones planted by Joshua in the midst of the river Jordan (Gen. 28:18, 19; Josh. 4:1-9). The meaning of the New Testament "remembrance" is related to the Old Testament memory. The Hebrew word *zakar* has all the concreteness of Hebrew thought behind it. In this sense we do not draw on fading occurrences, but re-present the singular historical Christ event in present effective action. This memory is sacred memory. At the Last Supper Jesus said, "The Comforter, who is the Holy Spirit, whom the Father will send in my name, he shall teach you all things, and *bring all things to your remembrance*" (John 14:26). The Church's record of the historical act of Christ is in itself merely memory of the past, but through the Holy Spirit this mere memory becomes *anamnesis,* the past made present reality.[33] The Holy Spirit never brings attention or directs worship to Himself, but to the truth of God in Christ (John 16:13). And thus remembrance is even more than sacred memory, for the Holy Spirit makes the Church sit together with Christ in heavenly places.

The eucharistic worship of the Christian faith must never exclude and must always include *anamnesis*, for the sacrifice of Christ once offered on the Cross has been accepted in glory. In the power of that singular sacrifice Christ ever lives, our high priest and perpetual intercessor, the continually accepted propitiation for our sins until the end of time. Therefore, by grace all that we need do, or can do, is to "Do this in remembrance of me," by His Spirit through faith.

The once-and-for-all sacrifice cannot be repeated in any semblance; therefore, our Eucharist must be in "remembrance." The Church Fathers described it as, "The flesh and blood of this sacrifice, before Christ's coming was promised in victims that were types; in the passion of Christ it was rendered up in very reality; since Christ's ascension it is celebrated in the sacrament of memorial."[34] Christ presents His sacrifice for us in perpetual intercession, and we can but offer "Our Thanksgiving." *Eucharistia.*

In the remembrance of the Eucharist there is not only a memory of thanksgiving of the past, but also the projection into the future. Paul indoctrinated the Corinthian Christians concerning this truth of the Lord's Supper: "For the tradition which I handed on to you came to me from the Lord himself who on the night of his arrest took bread, and after giving thanks to God, broke it and said, 'This is my body which is for you; this do as a memorial of me. . .' For every time ye eat the bread, and drink the cup, ye proclaim the death of the Lord until He comes" (I Cor. 11:23-26). The term "proclaim" is nearer the truth than "show," and may

[33] Cf. Torrance, *op. cit.,* p. 176.
[34] Augustine, *C. Faust.* 20:21.

even be given as "announce" or "recite." Whichever term is selected, the sense of the text is that the Eucharist is a "proclamation." Professor Torrance describes the proclamation as "The Church on earth is given in its eucharistic worship to *echo* the eternal intercession of Christ."[35] This living echo of Calvary is the intercession of the Church. The Eucharist is the resounding "Amen" within the Christian faith, the counterpart on earth to the eternal intercession of Christ in heaven. The proclamation of the Church is "Alleluia, blessing and honor and glory and power be unto him that sitteth upon the throne, and unto the Lamb for ever and ever" (Rev. 5:13).

The fellowship of Christians proclaims the Gospel in the world. In heaven is the reconciling Son before the Father interceding for man; on earth is the Church showing forth His reconciliation and proclaiming His mercy and grace. The proclamation in the Eucharist dare not be only to the Church, but also as a witness to the world. Just as the world comes to know God's love through the Christian Agape, so the world comes to know God's redeeming sacrifice through the Christian Eucharist. The Christian message to all mankind is proclaimed in the Eucharist.

"Do this" is an imperative command of Christ. However, the command is not like the shout of a superior officer, but like the beckoning call of the loving Savior. We *follow* the action in the Last Supper in the final analysis because of the Person, Jesus Christ. The Head of the Eucharist-memorial is always God in Christ. He is the chief actor in the drama of Holy Communion. The Christian in the Church triumphant has the memory of his suffering Savior and the hope of his crowned Christ, "Do this in remembrance of me!"

The Eschatological Nature of The Eucharist

The consummation of the Eucharist is immediately determined in the inauguration of the Eucharist. The celebration

[35] Torrance, *op. cit.*, p. 176.

of the Eucharist is only "till He come" (I Cor. 11:29). This eschatological nature of the coming again of Christ is evident in the Eucharist, with all its richness, and the Agape with all its love, and the Pedilavium with all its symbolic cleansing, will end with the consummation of the coming Christ. The Eucharist will pass away with the passing world and be displaced with the marriage supper of the Lamb. Man's need of earthen symbols will be ended, for we shall be "like Him" (I John 3:2). We will not only be like Him, but we will be with Him in the Holy Temple of the New Jerusalem. "I saw the holy city, the new Jerusalem coming down from God out of heaven . . . and I saw no temple in the city; for its temple was the sovereign Lord God and the Lamb" (Rev. 21:2, 22). Insofar as this future nature is now present in the Eucharist can it be described as eschatological.

When Jesus transformed the Old Covenant into the New Covenant of the Church He also related it with the Kingdom of God. "I tell you this: never again shall I drink from the fruit of the vine until that day that I drink it new in the Kingdom of God" (Mark 14:25). The new covenant nature of the Church finds its final meaning in the Kingdom of God. Every time the Eucharist is celebrated by the Church it is proclaiming its transitory nature in the eternal nature of the Kingdom of Heaven. In this sense the Eucharist has a cosmic scope, a sacred history running from eternity to eternity, with the historic Christ as its central and determinative point.

The *eschaton* has entered history and yet the end is still future. In the Eucharist the Church anticipates the marriage supper in the new temple of the New Jerusalem. This between the time is the paradox of the Christian faith, in that Christ has come and yet is still to come. The Church has been redeemed and yet looks toward and awaits the redemption of the body. The Christian looks back to the Christ event in which he partakes, and forward to the full participation in the Kingdom of God. Every Holy Communion service is a rehearsal and an anticipation of the final Messianic banquet in the

Kingdom of Heaven. This is the future "hope" that we experience in the celebration of the Eucharist.

The period of time between Pentecost and the *parousia*, in which the Church has its being, is provisional. This period of waiting is not caused by either the weakness or disinterest of God. In fact, it is God's *abiding* love that provides for this interim period in which the Eucharist is a symbol. For it is during this provisional period, by the "hiddenness" of Christ, that all men may be brought to the truth of the Gospel in the hope that they will respond in faith to Christ. When the veiled Christ in the Eucharist is unveiled in the *parousia*, then the eschatology in part shall be made complete by the sovereign will of God. The Church which ever receives its being anew through the Holy Spirit, as the new creation which is yet to be revealed as the *parousia*, lives in dynamic tension here and now on the very frontier of eternity.[36]

The genuine Christian faith must place itself into this nature of eschatology. Whenever the Church refuses to abide in this eschatological position, its Holy Communion becomes but a mere human institution. The Church must ever realize that it transcends itself, its means and symbols, that the continuance of the Church in the present historical framework ceases at the appearance of Christ at the *parousia*. The horizontal nature of the Church and the sacraments begins and ends with the vertical coming of Christ. The very fact that the Church was created when Christ broke into history should press upon us the fact that it is divine in origin, and destiny. Just as, at the Last Supper, Christ was more interested in the future glory than the present means to that glory, the Cross; so we, at the Holy Communion, should be more interested in the Christ who is coming again than the symbols representing that coming.

The Church's proclamation of the Eucharist is never to itself, but to the Cross of Christ in the past and the consum-

[36] Torrance, *op. cit.*, p. 171.

mation of Christ in the future. The Eucharist is but a sounding board re-echoing the truth of God in the historical Gospel and a mirror reflecting the triumph of God in the eternal Christ. In our pivotal position we witness that which He has done in the past and show forth that which He will do in the future. If we should emphasize the memory to the exclusion of the eschatological hope, we would lose our "pivot" and fall into Christian error. The Eucharist is a symbolic means of worshipping the Christ of the Cross, required by creatures of flesh and blood in a fallen world which are saved and yet await final salvation. This is the eschatological nature of the eucharistic symbols through which we worship Christ, our King. "For as often as ye eat this bread, and drink this cup, ye do proclaim the Lord's death *till he come*" (I Cor. 11:26).

In conclusion, Christian worship of the sacrifice of Christ in the Eucharist is the heart of the Church. The Christian Gospel is that the eternal Christ broke into the line of history, casting the anchor which forms the spanning arch between God and man. The Church, as His body, is ever dependent on His coming to it, rather than dependent upon its own merits and gifts offered to God. Abraham as our type brought his best, his beloved son Isaac, but at the last moment God provided His own offering, His only-begotten Son! Then, as now, it is always God's divine action on our behalf that provides our eternal salvation. The redeeming love of God is the heart of the Gospel, and the heart of the Eucharist.

The Eucharist is the great confessional act of the Church, not just the confession of sin, nor the confession of a faith, but the confession of a Savior and a salvation. The celebration of the Eucharist is the sacramental symbol of the Christ event: the incarnation, the cross, the resurrection, the ascension, and the coming again. It proclaims that "God was in Christ reconciling the world to himself, no longer holding men's sins against them" (II Cor. 5:19). Christ, our Lord, does continually become more real when by the Holy Spirit through faith we celebrate the Eucharist.

"So now, my friends, the blood of Jesus makes us free to enter boldly into the sanctuary by the new, living way which he has opened for us through the curtain, the way of his flesh. We have, moreover, a great priest set over the household of God; so let us make our approach in sincerity of heart and full assurance of faith, our guilty hearts sprinkled clean, our bodies washed with pure water" (Heb. 10:19-22). As worshippers of the living God and Father, we sing His praises; as believers in Jesus Christ, we preach His Gospel; as new creatures born into the family of God, we proclaim the redemption of the Cross of Christ. But even with these glorious means there comes a time when they fail to express the veiled mystery of Christ, our loving Savior. And in our stammering silence He says, "Do this," "Do this in remembrance of me."

"*Crown Him the Lord of Love.*
Behold His hands and side,
Rich wounds yet visible above,
In beauty glorified.
All hail, Redeemer, hail!
For Thou hast died for me.
Thy praise shall never, never fail
Throughout eternity."

Alleluia!

6

The Communion Symbols

HOLY COMMUNION WAS THE ORIGINAL SYMBOL OF THE CHRISTIAN faith. The Church "signed its name" by chiseling the symbol of the bread and cup into stone and by painting the Lord's Supper upon its walls. When the Christians were being hunted down as martyrs they identified themselves to one another by the symbols of Holy Communion. During the first three centuries after Easter Christians symbolized their faith by the eucharistic elements enshrined in the Love-feast. In the early Church the Cross was not so much a symbol, but a way of life and death. The Last Supper later became a principal subject of all forms of art, identifying the Church to the total Gospel of Christ.

The distinct character of the early brethren was formed by Holy Communion. Before the Church had an organization or a theologically trained ministry, the Holy Communion bonded them into a fellowship of love and faith. The Love-feast was at the center of its doctrine. The "Agape" was the heart of the brethren from which issued its life and witness. It was around the Lord's Supper that the early brethren learned about the body of Christ, and the cleansing from sin by Christ was learned and experienced by the brethren at Holy Communion.

Later in the history of the Church, the Cross became the strong symbol. The Cross has become the exclusive symbol of the Christian faith. The symbol of the Cross creates its own atmosphere, the atmosphere of heaven and earth, bringing eternity and time together in a timelessness that has meaning for all people of all lands in all generations. It has meaning and understanding for the educated and uneducated, the rich and poor, the philosopher and the physicists, the black man and the white man. It unites and divides. It divides all unbelievers from eternal life. It unites all believers in a way that neither doctrine nor denomination can ever unite. The symbol of the Cross expresses the Gospel of Christ without the limitations of words and the mental effort of understanding. The symbol of the Cross "speaks" the amazing love of God to every man.

Symbolism, in the Christian faith and the world, occupies an essential place. By using the hearing of the ear, the seeing of the eye, the tasting of the mouth, the touching of the fingers, and the feeling of the heart, man is brought into a spiritual dimension that is not otherwise possible. "The mysterious feeding of spirit upon Spirit is made more not less real by the Communion meal which drives home the practical truth of our creaturely dependence."[1] Material media help stimulate man to express his highest devotion to God in Christ. The Holy Communion vividly expresses the divine truth of God. This study is limited to the symbolism of the Pedilavium, the Love-feast, and the Eucharist. These symbols are appointed by God for Holy Communion. Thus it is vital that we consider and understand symbols in a study of the Holy Communion.

[1] Underhill, Evelyn, *Worship,* (New York: Harper & Bros., 1957), p. 25.

Generally we may define a symbol as one reality that is related to and expresses another reality, a material media that represents and suggests a spiritual reality. At the root of the term there is the concept of putting together, the relating of two realities where certain elements of each are found in the other. The symbol is the explicit elements of each found in the other. The symbol is the explicit of the implicit which is not explicable in any other way. Communion symbols are sensible media ordained to express the suprasensible sacrifice of Christ.

Creation A Symbolic Expression

In the broadest sense the whole universe is a symbolic expression of God. The creation is the divine expression, reaching its highest form in man who is in the image of God. Because God expressed Himself in this process of creation, it bears His stamp of identity, whereby Paul declared, "His visible attributes, that is to say, his everlasting power and deity, have been visible, ever since the world began, to the eye of reason, in the things he has made" (Rom. 1:20). The material universe explicitly expresses the implicit reality of God. Therefore, in this sense the Gospel can be described as a Cross nailed together in the beginning of creation, "The Lamb of God slain from the foundation of the world." "God creates and recreates in an orderly fashion, not in a series of jerks based on the faithfulness or unfaithfulness of the people of God, but in a continuing will so that all may know Him and abide in His everlasting love."[2]

The divine miracle of creation is something more than material; it is the expression of the divine nature. In stating that the whole universe expresses God, we must guard ourselves against any notion of a natural religion, a Stoic pantheism. In a previous chapter the distinction was made that God is not

[2] Wotherspoon, H. J., *Religious Values In The Sacraments,* (Edinburgh: T. & T. Clark, 1928), p. 8.

in time or space, for they are a part of His creation and therefore in Him. He is not in the particles of creation, for every particle of creation is His; matter does not possess Him for He possesses and controls all things. The Gnostic concept that the "soul of nature" is God, or vice versa, is alien to the Christian faith. In the book of Colossians, Paul laid bare the empty, false gospel of Gnosticism, which was no gospel (Col. 2:4, 8, 18, 21). God entered the realm of nature in the Person of Jesus Christ, and in Him alone is the union of God and the world. The "Logos" is not in the "Cosmos"; rather, the "Cosmos" is in the "Logos."

The Hebrew people had a sovereign view of nature. The writers of the Old Testament bear witness that God is sovereign in heaven and earth. To them the peaceful, pastoral seasons and the violent upheavals of earth were all a part of the sovereign will of God. God spoke to man through the medium of nature which expressed His love and His judgment. The Hebrews more than any other people reflected upon the natural happenings: the drought, the famine, the seasons, the harvest, and the storms that came upon themselves and their enemies. But whatever the circumstance, they were convinced that *Yahweh* was determining His will and was in all things.

The Christian view of nature is based upon the revelation of God in the Person of Jesus Christ, for in Christ there is criterion and fulfillment. The Hebrew knew that calm and storm, flood and fertility were in the sovereign will of God for judgment and redemption. However, it was in Christ that the parable of the grain falling into the ground which dies and brings new life became meaningful. Vegetation fades and dies in the autumn, but the garment of nature is renewed to life in the spring; the storm leaves destruction in its trail but it is most often the prelude to new life. Symbols of gain-through-loss and of life-through-death abound in the realm of nature. The yielding of Jesus Christ to the hardwood of the Cross and making His grave in the rock-hewn tomb stand for all time as the divine way of gain-through-loss and life-through-death. In His death and resurrection nature's ultimate riddle, death, was redeemed.[3] "O death where is thy sting? O grave where is thy victory" (I Cor. 15:55). By this supreme act of God in the earth all nature becomes meaningful in the symbolic character of the will and love of God.

The whole natural universe which repeats and re-echoes the spiritual is localized in man. We who are in the image of God understand both the explicit of nature and the implicit of spirit; we see God in creation and hear His Eternal Spirit who speaks to our spirits. We understand both because we are composed of both material and spiritual. A comprehensive view of man is that he is a part of nature and at the same time transcends nature. Self stands at the juncture of spirit and nature. The light of the world and the truth in our hearts is more than analogy; it is identity connoting one another. Likewise, the darkness in the world and evil in men's hearts are more than fanciful language; they are physical symbols speaking a spiritual reality, or nonreality. In the world a straight line somehow signifies just action and righteousness, just as a crooked line depicts the ways of crooked men. And when man uses nature for evil and self-destruction, it reveals the sin in the heart of man, rather than evil in the heart of nature. "Bad men all hate the light and avoid it for fear their practices should be shown up. The honest man comes to the light so that it may be clearly seen that God is in all he does" (John 3:20, 21).

In all of our human exprience the outward and the inward, the material and the spiritual are bound together. We ourselves are souls in bodies and we use material means to express our mentally conceived purposes, and language to express our thoughts. "Symbols are distinguished from instruments in that symbols are known by what is known by them, while instru-

[3] Cf. Dillstone, F. W., *Christianity and Symbolism*. (London: Collins, 1955), p. 69.

ment gets its definition by what is done to it."[4] The human body is more than a simple instrument, either of oneself or of another being, but is the symbolic expression of one's soul. Jesus taught this relationship when he said, "But what comes out of the mouth has its origins in the heart; and that is what defiles a man. Wicked thoughts, murder, adultery, fornication, theft, perjury, slander – these all proceed from the heart; and these are the things that defile a man; but to eat without first washing his hands, that cannot defile him" (Matt. 15:18-20). Evil which is suggested to us from outside is simply cast off like mud from the bottom of our shoes, unless it meets with some response from within. Likewise the Gospel of God that is spoken to the person falls on deaf ears unless there is some response from within.

The spiritual is always seeking a physical expression, such as harmony in music, beauty in art, and love in marriage. On the human level, if the "spiritual" reality cannot find a physical expression it dies. As has been said, the soul cannot ever be found naked; it is always making for itself body, clothing itself in fōrm, developing for itself a means of action.[5] The spirit needs some form in any realm in order to be able to express itself. Thus we can understand Paul's teaching concerning the physical and spiritual body, "But God giveth it a body as it has pleased him, and to every seed his own body. . . There are celestial bodies, and bodies terrestrial" (I Cor. 15:38, 40). As the celestial and terrestrial bodies of man have a glory in expression, so in a sense we can understand the universe as a vehicle of God symbolizing His power, harmony, beauty, and love. This concept of the external world being the outward symbol expression of God removes any charge of magic, any idea of pantheism, and any notion of sacerdotalism in the sacramental symbols of the Christian faith.

[4] Quick, O. C., *The Christian Sacraments,* (London: Nisbitt and Company, 1927), p. 1.

[5] Wotherspoon, *op. cit.,* p. 9.

Calvin taught that God continually revealed Himself and His divine truth through symbols. Repeatedly, in the Old Testament, God used symbols to communicate to men and, at the same time, obscure the intensity of His glory. Calvin called not only the ark and the burning bush symbols of the presence of God, but also the cloud and smoke and flame and other accompanying phenomena as the symbols of his expression. These phenomena were called symbols of celestial glory, as veils behind which God stands in revealing Himself to men. God is described as wrapping Himself up in many folds, in symbolic means, so that men might hear without being stricken by His glory.[6] God veiled and unveiled Himself in His holy communications with men. The ultimate and supreme veiling and unveiling of God to man were in His incarnate Son, Jesus Christ. ". . . bearing the human likeness, revealed in human shape" (Phil. 2:8).

Faith Needs Symbols

The Christian faith demands symbols. We can begin by saying that God is, or that God is being without using any symbolic language. This simply states positively the actuality of God, implying the negative, that non-being would not be God. This is implicit in our faith and is the foundation for everything in our faith that is acted or articulated. However, the implicit of God must be made explicit if there is to be communication, revelation, between God and man. Jesus Christ is the revelation of God, in whom all of life is symbolized. "When in former times God spoke to our forefathers, he spoke in fragmentary and varied fashion through the prophets. But in this the final age he has spoken to us in the Son whom he has made heir to the whole universe, and through whom he created all orders of existence; the Son who is the *effulgence* of God's splendour and the *stamp*

[6] Cf. Wallace, R. S., *Calvin's Doctrine of the Word and Sacrament,* (Edinburgh: Oliver and Boys, 1953), p. 5.

of God's very being . . ." (Heb. 1:1-3). As Professor McIntyre writes, "Insofar as we think at all we must think in human terms; only God can think of Himself in other terms. So anthropomorphic thinking about God in some form must be inescapable. Anthropomorphism begins to be an error, when we picture God's being too much in terms of human emotions, instability, narrowness of sympathy and love, or even in rather crude physical categories. The conception of the deities in the Graeco-Roman religion would be an example of the wrong type of anthropomorphism."[7] The incarnation of Jesus Christ into a certain period of history, into a world of life, of work, of friendships, of death, and of resurrection from the dead has taught us rightly how to think of God in human symbols.

In the teaching ministry of our Lord there was the simple truth in precept, "Blessed are the pure in spirit for they shall see God." More often, however, the Lord taught the deep divine truths of God in symbolic parables from nature. The parable chapter in Matthew is filled with this symbolic teaching (Matt. 13). The reception of the Gospel in the hearts of men is likened to the reception of seed in the soil. In this the implicit truth of the various conditions of the heart of man is evident in the explicit condition of the soil. The parable of the tares in the wheat is the symbolic expression of evil in God's world, implicit truth in explicit nature. Jesus likened the Kingdom of God to the small mustard seed which grew big enough for birds to roost among its branches. Also the yeast in flour is a symbol teaching of the explicit growth from the implicit element. Then the Gospel of Matthew gives the meaning of parables in the prophecy, "I will utter things kept secret since the world was made" (Ps. 78:2). Christ used the explicit natural world to express the implicit truth of God.

[7] McIntyre, John, *On The Love of God,* (London: Collins, 1962), p. 58.

The Gospel of John is distinct by signs and by the teaching of the Lord that is symbolic in character. The Lord taught in John, chapter fifteen, that the vine and branches are symbols of the relationship of Christ and His disciples. Throughout the allegory it is clearly understood that Christ is the vine and the disciples are the branches in a metaphorical sense. This symbolism has a rich background which gives it deep meaning. Isaiah uses the symbol of the vine as the people of God planted into a nation by Jehovah (Isa. 5:1-7). The Psalmist depicts the history of Israel from the exodus as the clearing of a vineyard, transplanting the vine, the rich growth, the neglect, and the transplanting it receives from transgression (Ps. 80:9-15). The prophet Jeremiah proclaims that the fine vine that he planted was degenerate (Jer. 2:21). From this Old Testament background and from the common experience of everyday vineyards, the disciples understood the inner significance of this symbolic teaching. In fact, the symbolism of the vine and branches is almost absorbed into the reality of the relationship of Christ and His disciples. In this natural, simple way Christ taught one of the supreme divine truths, our life in God. In a similar way the symbol of water has an old and rich background in the ceremonial cleansing of the priests in the service of God; as such it is used in the washing of the disciples' feet (John 13).

In the Gospel of John not only the teachings are symbolic in character, but also the miracles and acts had both an external and inner meaning. The cleansing of the temple not only brought order to Jerusalem's temple, but also symbolized the continual cleansing of the Father's house in all time. The healing of the blind not only gave physical sight to some people of Palestine, but also symbolized the spiritual sight that is given to all who are touched by the Lord. The raising of Lazarus is most certainly a symbolic teaching of His own resurrection. Professor C. H. Dodd writes, "The narrative of John is at the same time factually true and symbolic of a deeper truth, since things and events in this world derive what reality they possess from the eternal ideas they embody. John writes in terms of a world in which phenomena – things and events – are a living and moving image of the eternal, and not a veil of illusion to hide it, a world in which the Word is made flesh."[8]

When teaching is in precept we can ponder, be perplexed, and be passive. But when the teaching is in the form of symbolic character, the whole realm of nature presses upon us and penetrates our whole beings. Teaching in symbolic parables informs our minds, stirs our emotions, and often moves our wills. The will of man which is basic to our moral and spiritual life is more often moved by a natural symbol than by an abstract precept. In contrast to precept teaching the parable gives the motivation to act upon the truth it declares. In the symbolic parable we not only understand the inner truth, but also "see" it in undeniable evidence.

The prophets of the Old Testament employed symbols to express their prophecy. The weight of their messages was too much for words to carry, and they used the practical symbol in a way distinctive to the eastern mind. Jeremiah prophesied destruction and oppression by laying a yoke on his shoulders (Jer. 27:2; 2:28:10). Isaiah symbolized the shameless, naked power of Assyia to Israel by loosing his sackcloth and removing his shoes as he walked among the people (Isa. 20). Abijah rent his garment into ten pieces to express the rending of the kingdom (I Kings 11:30). Hosea proclaimed the infidelity of Israel by a symbolic marriage of infidelity. These prophets of Israel proclaimed the message of God in these unique symbolic ways, and combined with prophetic conviction they expressed the divine truth to the nation and to the generations.

A religion of faith and prayer must have a structure of

[8] Dodd, C. H., *Interpretation of the Fourth Gospel,* (Cambridge: University Press, 1953), p. 140.

physical expressions. The expressions in our faith take the form of Biblical narratives and worship. These are the objective and subjective sides of the same reality. An illustration may help to clarify the truth of the symbolic in the Christian faith: When we tell our children about God we say He is our heavenly Father. These very words are symbolic of a certain imaginative act, and this imaginative act reveals to the child a more or less elderly person somewhere out of sight. This is certainly not the *meaning* of the child's faith in God; this is the symbolism. Now when we are teaching our children in this way, we do not say that this is imagery and not literally true and that they must interpret the symbols in a spiritual sense. For the child will naturally interpret the symbols in a spiritual sense. The child, more often than an adult, has no problem of understanding the implicit in the explicit, the spiritual in the material. *The truth grows up within a scaffolding of symbols; deprive the child of symbols and it will never grow!*[9] Lose the symbol and you will lose the meaning as well. Christian symbols express divine truth in our faith and they are fundamental in our worship of God in Christ.

Although symbols are necessary in our worship, yet they must necessarily "fade away," and they are never to be the end of our faith. In the symbols we strive for the innermost reality; at the moment the inner meaning is realized, the symbol itself fades into a valueless background. However, as the distinction between the implicit reality and the explicit symbol is not always discerned, the symbol rather than what it symbolizes takes on religious value. Often the implicit truth and the explicit symbol are so closely fused that the divine worth of the spiritual reality is transferred to the symbol; hence, very often in our Christian faith the symbol rather than the truth it expresses becomes sacred.

As long as the world remains, as long as Christian worship

[9] Collingwood, R. G., *Speculum Mentis,* (Oxford: Clarendon Press, 1924), p. 122.

involves a considerable number of spoken words and visual symbols, as it inevitably must do, there is a constant risk that the symbol becomes the idol, the substitute figure for the reality who is God. As long as the presence of God is realized by the Holy Spirit in ordinary men and women, it is involved with their volitions and emotions. However, as the Holy Spirit draws one near to the reality, the human volition and emotions fuse into the divine will and pure love of God. It is constantly and always the love of God through the Holy Spirit that preserves the spiritual truth of God in the material world in which we live.

In addition to the constant danger of the symbol becoming sacred instead of the inner reality it symbolizes, in the opposite and most interesting experience, the vitally interested individual comes in conflict with religion itself. For when an individual diligently seeks the implicit truth and discovers it for himself, he immediately begins to take the "symbolic scaffolding" away, or to speak about it lightly and with little reverence. It has served its purpose in his life and he is willing, and often anxious, to discard it. This is one reason why some very genuinely spiritual people often shock slightly spiritual people by their irreverent attitudes toward religious traditions. However, it is vital to keep the Christian symbols expressing the divine truth, not only for those who have not perceived the implicit truth as yet, but also for those who have come to the spiritual reality in the symbols, that they may have means to express their faith.

The term "symbol" is used in this study of the Holy Communion in preference to the term "sign." We believe that the term symbol connotes the explicit expressions in a way superior to and nearer the intention of God than the term "sign." First of all, let us distinguish the symbol from the sign by the following description. The symbol represents; the sign indicates. The symbol expresses indirectly; the sign transmits directly. The symbol reminds or refers to; the sign announces. The symbol extends the teaching of the truth indefinitely; the sign operates in the immediate context of space and time.[10] One of the most important of the differences of the symbol and the sign is that the symbol bears a relationship to what it symbolizes, while the sign bears no necessary relation to that which it points. The symbol in a way participates in the reality of that for which it stands; the sign is arbitrarily designed by the necessity of expediency. From this description of the symbol, it has already become evident that the symbols of the Lord's Supper express the grace and power of God in a way that cannot be lightly discerned or rightly discarded. The symbols of the Holy Communion were instituted to express in our human life the divine life that we have in our Lord Jesus Christ.

In this section on Christian symbolism, it has become clear and evident that symbols are vital to our daily living faith and Christian worship. Language is very often ambiguous and unable to express fully the deeper divine truths of God. Language at best is necessarily composed from the known and, therefore, capable of expressing only what is already known. The weakness of language is thus twofold: it is incapable of revealing the unknown, and it is not sufficient as a sole means of prayer and of praising God. Paul wrote, "In the same way the Spirit comes to the aid of our weakness. We do not even know how we ought to pray, but through our inarticulate groans the Spirit himself is pleading for us, and God who searches our inmost being knows what the Spirit means, because he pleads for God's own people in God's own way . . ." (Rom. 8:26).

Realities which come to us through the sense of sight sink deeper than those received by the sense of hearing. The symbols of Holy Communion which employ our senses of touch, taste, hearing, and sight are impressed still deeper into our lives. A man is not a soul and a body; he is one being, and through the body the soul realizes itself. Christian sym-

[10] Cf. Dillstone, *op. cit.*, p. 24.

bols are the natural way to "speak" and reveal the implicit truth of God. In our Christian communion the symbols express the sense of things; they show the inner truth that is real to our souls. The symbol can be perceived by people of all cultures and is apprehensible in all generations. What more can be spoken about the divine cleansing than, "He took a towel and girded himself and began to wash his disciples' feet"? What lengthy discourse would more adequately describe the divine love in the family of God than the Lovefeast? How long would it take to say in words what is said about the sacrifice of Christ for the atonement of man in the bread and cup? Words fail thought, and we are driven for expression to the symbolic; without it the higher brain is dumb. Christ said, "*Do this* in remembrance of me," a symbolic action. In communion God has provided the means for human creatures to experience and perceive the glorious Gospel of Jesus Christ.

Christianity is much more than teaching and preaching; it is contact with the living God through Christ. It is man's response to the love and call of God. In Holy Communion this contact is not dependent upon or hindered by any human agency, such as a teacher or preacher; it is directly apprehensible and immediately operative. One of the sterling truths of the faith is that the essence of Christianity is not dogma, but the communion of man with God. *Holy Communion is not talk about God, but the experience of the spiritual Person, power and reality of God.* We meet Him in Person, not precept. Like the man of old we declare, "I beheld the glory of the Lord."

Communion Symbols Unalterable

Are the Christian sacramental symbols of bread, wine, and water, which were derived from an agrarian society, really meaningful in our scientific society? The question is meaningful when it is recognized that our way of life has changed whereby many symbols of life have been lost in the transition. Churches of America, and of the world, have become churches of the city. People in these cities have no vivid view of nature, or they have adopted the view of nature as something to be simply utilized and exploited. People of the city almost regard rain as a curse because it ruins vacation and recreation plans. This view of nature reduces the meaning of Christian symbols to their lowest status. The further man moves away from the "land" the further he moves from the natural setting of bread and water, sheep and shepherd, seed and sower, vine and branches, and other great symbols of nature which are the bearers of spiritual meaning. Man, in our age of scientific technology, dispenses with nature and its symbols, or designs one from the transitory life on a temporary basis.

There is an increasingly greater contrast between the previous agrarian cultures and our technological society. Water has become almost hidden or highly artificial in water mains under the pavements; it is controlled by commissions and can be bought regardless of drought. What a contrast between agrarian people of old who looked to God for rain to cleanse and sustain, and modern man who looks to government or other men to supply his needs. The symbolic significance of the home has changed from an abiding place of love and shelter to a station in which to refill and from which to run. The symbolic character of the father wanes from a teacher and guardian of life to a silent provider. The parent plays an ever-diminishing role in family life; whereas, the nursery-school and teacher-professor assume the responsibility for the training and bringing up of the child. The symbolism of fire loses its appeal with the loss of the presence of fire in heating and cooking. Fire is now chiefly the hidden agent to release energy for technology purposes. With the coming of the atomic age, the symbol of fire has changed from a servant to warm our homes and cook our food, to a master that threatens all mankind. Birth and death and rebirth have little significance within a mechanical society. Of course there are still vast areas of the world that are predominantly agrarian. However, the rapid mechanization of agriculture and the standardization of planning have also changed their ways of life. The parable of the seed and sower does not mean the same thing to the man operating powerful machines as it did to the man working with simple tools.

Above all these changes is the change in rapid transportation and communication of modern man. The past generation has experienced a greater change in communication and transportation than all previous generations. From the time of Abraham to the time of George Washington, people simply wrote with many of the same materials, and traveled in the same manner and at the same speed. With homemade quills and ink they penned their messages on parchments that were delivered on foot. Today, with such instruments as the telstar, messages can be beamed around the world in an instant of time. This means that the patterns and purposes of the technological age have laid hold of the human mind to an extent which would have seemed impossible before.

These changes which have been noted are but illustrations of a changing way of life. However, many other generations have had major changes in their way of life, and every generation is in some degree unique. We recognize that all of man's history is perspective. There is no absolute basis by which we can describe or analyze the change in our way of life. Change from what? There is no other human society which provides a norm. We can say with certainty only that we are different in ways from the previous generation, and the emerging generation. In this sense, therefore, the changes that are occurring are minimized and appear even less significant from the historical vantage point of God.

Changes that do occur in a culture are not always away from that which has gone before. Sometimes there is a cycle of change whereby a society returns to positions and beliefs previously held. To a degree this has occurred in our technological society: "The present period is one in which a major effort is being made in the scientific world to restore a sense of proportion and balance which had almost been lost. The efficiency of the machine is undoubted . . . but the operator must also be considered."[11] This is demonstrated in our age of science where the "electronic brain" is dependent upon a constructor and stimulator. The constructor and operator of the machine must be considered in relation to the total purpose of the machine age. One might say that it is no longer the physical sciences that sit solely in the seat of control of our society. The presence of the experimenter does affect the results of the experiment. In other words, the subjective element is evident and accountable even in science. Therefore, since the subjective approach to our Christian faith cannot be concluded as nonvalid, there is a new appreciation of self in the world.

Now, more specifically, what is the status of the symbols used in Holy Communion? Although water has become more and more artificial in our way of life, yet it is still essential in every stage of life, in the beginning of individual existence and in the continuance of that existence. Water is still the basic life-giving and body-cleansing element in our world: its value in life and the world will grow when the fresh water supply becomes more acute with the growing population of the world. Thus water, as a symbol of cleansing in baptism and the Pedilavium, is relevant today. The effectiveness of this symbol will grow when our attention is directed more to the basic rite of cleansing. Let it be taught that the symbolic act of washing is that of the Triune God — Father, Son, and Holy Spirit, who creates and sustains and purifies the life of the whole universe. The water should be recognized as a symbol by which God shows us again and again His purging power, to refresh us by a renewed realization of the cleansing of our dirty, guilty souls from sin.

[11] Dillstone, *op. cit.*, p. 293.

In relation to the Eucharist the symbolism of the bread and the cup is real and vivid in all cultures. The grain of wheat must still be buried in the ground and die, or it abides alone; the fruit of the vine must still be crushed if it is to be transformed into the cup of blessing. In all the world, whatever the nature of culture, bread in some form is still the most common item of food. Bread is still the staff of life, and the breaking of bread is the act and entrance to that life. Therefore, there is no semblance of reason why bread should not be a most effective symbol in the Eucharist. Its symbolic meaning will be made relevant when it is taught to be the common that is made sacred by the act of God in Christ. Regardless of whether it be an urban or agrarian people the symbol of the "bread which we break" is powerful in meaning. Certainly even the technician or factory-worker, living in the heart of a city, who *sees* the bread which is consecrated to God, who beholds and "tastes" the sacramental bread now made available for him, cannot fail to perceive in some sense the Christ who died for him, and the God who sustains all life. The symbol of bread remains the symbol of life in all generations.

The cup of blessing in the Eucharist remains a superb symbolic expression of the sealing of the New Covenant. Since the breach in life in the dawn of history between Cain and Abel, there has been the symbol of the covenant to cement the two parties together in a bond of peace. Twentieth-century man is just as much as ever giving his blood in the battles of war in the vain effort of eliminating the animosities of the world and cementing the love among men. Certainly our generation should understand the meaning of shedding blood. Just as certainly, the truth should dawn on our generation that the blood that avails is the blood of Jesus Christ! The giving and receiving of His blood for the atonement of our sins in the New Covenant is the sacramental symbol of the cup of blessing that shall never wax old. Whether we live in Washington or Moscow, in the city or on the farm, in the first century or the twentieth century, the blood of Jesus

Christ remains symbolized in the cup of blessing. When we lift the cup of blessing in Holy Communion we realize anew our being lifted from sin to salvation, from the old creation to a new creation by the Lord Jesus Christ. Time does not touch this symbol of the cup in the Eucharist of Holy Communion.

Not only because water, bread, and the cup of blessing have specific ordained qualities, but also because of their particular symbolic nature, the sacramental symbols of the Christian faith pierce through time and culture to penetrate the soul of man. They possess a timeless quality that transcends the flux of mankind. They are most powerful in presenting the truth of God in Christ through all generations. They endure true sacramental symbols expressing the mighty act of God in Christ for all people of all time.

The sacramental symbols of Holy Communion are unalterable not only because they are based on institution, but also because of their congruity with the things they signify. In other words, sacramental symbols were not arbitrarily selected, depending solely upon divine fiat. They do carry the signature and authority of God, but this signature was placed upon something that had the character and quality of that signature. Christ elected the symbols that had representing character: water for cleansing, supper for communal life in the family of God, broken bread for His broken body which spanned the breach between man and God, and red wine for the red blood that was shed for the atonement of sin. Whatever else they might be, the sacraments of Holy Communion are first of all symbolic, representing as well as applying. Therefore, just as they were arbitrarily chosen so they can not be arbitrarily replaced. *To tamper with a symbol is to modify its testimony, just as to change the Word of God is to change the doctrine of God.* If all that has been said about the sacraments being a testimony to Christ is true, then they are as unalterable as the heavenly things they signify.

We have seen the unalterable character of the sacramental

symbols of Holy Communion in external evidences; now we shall consider the more vital internal evidences. The symbols of Holy Communion are permanent and unalterable because of their meaning and content. In Holy Communion Christ has instituted and erected at the center of the Church· pillars of witness on which He has inscribed His Gospel. The faith exercised in coming to the table of the Lord, is faith in the Lord. The Person of Christ gives meaning and eternal value to the sacramental symbols. Perhaps we can make it plain by an illustration of a check.[12] The value of a check has no relation to the paper upon which it is written; but its face value is the writing on it and the signature attached to it. If that is good, the worth is face value. However, if the writing is altered, it will not be honored, even with the name still inscribed (cf. Matt. 7:21-29).

Holy Communion, more than we realize, more than any other piece of "religious equipment," draws us to the Cross and compels us to bow before the Lord. It compels in us a faith – not a faith in an institution, not faith in a doctrine of atonement, or even faith in faith itself, but in the Person of Jesus Christ. There is the Person of Christ whom we apprehend by the symbols which represent His mighty act: incarnation, crucifixion, resurrection, and *parousia*. They bring us to an open faith in Him, which in turn takes us far into the unseen. Therefore, to attempt to change the means which He instituted, or the character which is His Person, would destroy their very essence and value. Christian sacraments of the Holy Communion are as unalterable as the eternal Christ. Zwingli wrote, "We venerate and cherish the symbols of sacred things, not as if they were themselves or the things of which they are signs. . . But through the symbols Christ Himself is, as it were, present to our eyes, so that not only the ears but the eyes and mouth may discern the Christ

[12] Cf. Wotherspoon, p. 24.

whom the soul has present within and rejoices in."[13] Holy Communion and the Person of Christ are inextricably interwoven, not only in their institution but also by their apprehension by man, for as a man thinketh about Holy Communion, so he will think about Christ. If he has a base concept of Holy Communion he will have a base concept of Christ. If he has a high concept of Holy Communion he will have a high concept of the Person of Christ. In this sense Holy Communion is the real theology of the common man; it guards his Gospel and guides him by it to the throne of God. The language of the pulpit and the Church is sometimes foreign to the ears of the uninitiated, but the language of Holy Communion speaks loud and clear in a universal language concerning the Christ who loved and saved all who will come and "sup with the Lord." The emphasis of the Church varies, and needs to vary, when the needs of the world around it vary. However, the sacramental symbols remain the same constant means to Christ our Lord. Man may criticize the action of the Church, but never the acts of Holy Communion. Holy Communion is the "mind" of the Church which keeps in store the truth and knowledge of God in Christ. It by no means displaces Holy Scriptures, but depicts them that all may see, and touch, and taste the wonder of our Christ.

The history of the Church reveals that at times it has not kept the faith pure in its clarion call. It was during these times that Holy Communion preserved and presented to common man the truths of God in the Gospel. They remain the changeless criterion upon which all theology is tested and found true, or wanting. In Holy Communion is the embodiment of the Gospel of God which gives the acid test to all doctrine and theology. The Gospel is a story told in symbols. "The theologian must not alter either the story or the symbols;

[13] Zwingli, *Fidei Expositio,* Eng. 2.240.

his task is to show how they mediate God's love and grace."[14] Holy Communion is a theology that never needs revising or reprinting!

Holy Communion summarizes, enshrines and safeguards the Gospel. There is a continuing development and change, not only in the way of life, but in the mind of man. In the philosophies of the world which cradle the mind of man in the world, there were the hellenistic mind, the medieval mind, the scholastic mind, the rational mind, the scientific mind, and now the cosmic mind. All of these philosophies had their direct and indirect effect upon not only the mind of the people outside the Church, but also the "mind" of the Church itself. In this changing pattern of thinking there is always the persistent danger of the synthesis of pagan philosophies with the Christian faith. But in Holy Communion Christ proclaims that He is the author and finisher of our faith. He brings all men to the heart of the matter, their sin and His sacrifice and salvation. The practice of Holy Communion acts like an anchor that holds the vessel in position while the gales blow and the tides come and go.

The Christian faith is a religion with a teacher (*didaskalos*), learners (*mathetas*), and a textbook (*bibliou*). Christianity definitely does have an intellectual teaching side to it, an objective reality in the Gospel that must be articulated. "How can they have faith in one they had never heard of? And how hear without someone to spread the news" (Rom. 10:14)? The Church does by divine commission employ the method of teaching and preaching the Gospel of Christ. However, in the worship at Holy Communion there is an individual communion with God that transcends all other methods. The power of Holy Communion is self-evident, unfettered from all human limitations.

Man's seeking of the love, grace, and power of God often

[14] Owen, H. P., *Revelation and Existence,* (Cardiff: University of Wales Press, 1957), p. 153.

results in ceremonial color, ecclesiastical externals, or dogmatic detail incomprehensible to the common man. The Gospel of love, grace, and power of God in Christianity comes to us in a holy simplicity in Holy Communion. Holy Communion is a simple act and comes to us in this life and world in as purely spiritual sense as possible. This act of God is made apprehensible by sacramental symbols, symbols that have a character and relevancy created by Christ. Man comes to the table of the Lord with simple faith and full surrender. His hands are empty; he brings nothing but repentance and faith. But in his emptied hands God will place His offering, the body and blood of His Son, our Lord Jesus Christ. In Holy Communion is the loving encounter of the heavenly Father with His adopted children, the family of God.

The Christian symbols in the sacrament of Holy Communion are endowed with spiritual meaning. The symbols of the water, the supper, the bread and cup have a revelancy today which comfort and confirm the believer, and confront and convert the unbeliever. The Christian symbols are a universal language speaking to the souls of Asian and African, European and American. They speak the truth of God in ancient and modern cultures, in changing times. The Christian symbols are the bulwarks in the teaching of the Church, never failing. The symbols of the Christian faith cohere in the living Christ in heavenly places, "till He comes."

7

The Price of Life

ALL SINCERE CHRISTIANS HAVE A DEEP DESIRE FOR HOLY COMMUNION with God. The sacred drama of Holy Communion draws us irresistibly to the very center of God. This compelling desire issues from the love of God at Golgotha. The Self-giving of God is unforgettable and begets sacrifice in us. The price of His love moves us to surrender our human pride and pay the price of true Communion. Just as loving moves others to love, so sacrifice begets sacrifice, and in the use of the sacred symbols of Communion which are a reminder of His sacrifice men and women are persuaded to dedicate themselves anew to God, whatever the personal price may be. The price is sacrifice, the prize is true Communion with the living God. Communion is the proclamation of Good Friday and Easter Sunday – the price and the prize.

Bought At A Price

The Apostle Paul says, "ye are bought at a price" (I Cor. 6:20). Christian faith is free, but not cheap. Our eternal life cost God the life of His only begotten Son. The price of Holy

Communion is Christ who made Himself nothing and assumed the flesh of sinful man. The love of the Father moved Him to give His Son who for our sake became an accursed thing on the Cross. God's salvation for man was costly because it cost God His all. The supreme value of the Christian faith cannot be measured by instrument in hand or sense of mind; it can only be reflected in His incarnation and crucifixion.

The costly Christian grace is contrasted with the cheap grace that is presumed and practiced by multitudes who lay claims to Him. As the Christian martyr of Nazi Germany, Dietrich Bonhoeffer, poignantly describes it, "Cheap grace means grace sold on the market like cheapjack's wares. The sacraments, the forgiveness of sin, and the consolations of religion are thrown away at cut prices. Grace is represented as the Church's inexhaustible treasury, from which she showers blessings with generous hands, without asking questions or fixing limits. Grace without price, grace without cost! The essence of grace, we suppose, is that the account has been paid in advance; and, because it has been paid, everything can be had for nothing. Since the cost is infinite, using and spending it are infinite."[1]

A story which illustrates the cost of salvation and Holy Communion is that of the Christian layman in a mining town. The Christian had, over a period of time, befriended a miner, and taught him the simple essence of the Gospel. He described the sinfulness of man and his utter helplessness to save himself from sin. The Christian taught that the Holy God demands holiness, but the demand has been provided for in Jesus Christ. He taught about the incarnation, crucifixion, resurrection, and coming again of Christ, and that salvation is the gift of God through faith – the Gospel. One day the layman met the friend, at the entrance of the mine shaft, and as they walked together asked him if he were not ready to put

[1] Bonhoeffer, Dietrich, *The Cost of Discipleship,* (London: SCM, 1959), p. 35.

his faith in Jesus Christ. The friend replied that he had come to the point of wanting the salvation of God but thought that the Christian Gospel was too cheap. It seemed too easy, too simple to be real. The Christian turned and asked the friend how he had come out of the dark, dirty mine to the surface, to the light, to the fresh air, to his home again? The miner replied, "By the mine lift, of course." The Christian layman asked him, "How much did it cost you?" The miner replied, "Why nothing, it is the company's!" "Yes," replied the layman, "but it cost the company all it had. Because you rode up free does not make it cheap, rather it means that the cost has been paid by the Company!"

The church stands indicted of making "free" grace "cheap." We stand upon the truth of free justification by faith alone (cf. Rom. 3:23), excluding any serious attempt at dedicated Christian discipleship (cf. Rom. 1:15-19). The doctrine of justification has been separated from the corollary doctrine of sanctification to the point where they are not only strangers to the Christian, but almost enemies. The Church has naively preached the grace of God for the sins of man, forgetting the "sinning believer." Or perhaps it was not naiveté so much as pure indulgence in sin while assuming shelter under the religious umbrella of cheap grace. "Cheap grace is the preaching of forgiveness without requiring repentance, Baptism without Church discipline, Holy Communion without confession, absolution without personal confession. Cheap grace is grace without discipleship, grace without the Cross, grace without Jesus Christ, living and incarnate."[2] The price for the pardon of our sins was and is Christ crucified. The cost of Holy Communion is the Cross of Christ. Thus that which had an infinite cost has an infinite value and demands our uttermost in faith and practice.

The Church has come to the point of common acceptance by "Christian Society," whereby the distinctiveness of Chris-

[2] Bonhoeffer, *op. cit.,* p. 36.

tian discipleship has been lost. With the presence of the Church everywhere the realization of the price of its "Cornerstone" has faded. The cost of the life of the Head of the Church has been absorbed into institutionalism. As the world became Christianized, the Church became secularized, and grace became its common property. The Church has assumed a corner on the market of Christian grace, and sells it for a price. As the demand declines, the price becomes cheap. The price of Christian grace has declined to the point of "The Protestant Hour" on Sunday morning. The respectable Christian needs only to take one hour out of his secular life to go to Church and be assured that his sin has been forgiven through the Cross of Christ. However, the truth of the matter is that the spread of the Gospel doesn't spread the cost. The cost remains, through time and eternity, the single life of the Son of God. The Church is the body of Christ, the living body of the living Savior, who *continually* gives of *Himself* in Christian grace.

The meaning and value of God's grace in Holy Communion are determined by the Cross of Christ. If Christ is but the highest example of humanism, or if the Cross is but the supreme expression of martyrdom, then the sacrament of Communion can be redesigned or dismissed without consequence; but if God was in Christ and if the Cross was the crucial action of judgment grace, then the Holy Communion "in remembrance of Him" has eternal consequence. When we find Him to be our Lord and Redeemer, taking away the sin of the world, we will lend as much emphasis in the preparation and practice of Holy Communion as He did in preparing and practicing the Last Supper. We must fully realize that as He approached the Messianic summit, He designed and deliberately instituted the sacred rite that was to be practiced by the Christian community "till He comes again." Holy Communion must be kept in the context of the Person and work of Jesus Christ, the Son of God.

The resurrection and Pentecost kindled the disciples with

the divine knowledge that the gift of His death conveyed by the supper was eternal life. So convinced was the early Christian community of the essential value of Holy Communion for their life and faith that the records are filled with its practice in Christian martyrdom. At one time in this history the Christians were forced with the decision to say, "I confess," or apostatize. For the "Confessors" who awaited execution in the imperial prisons, the Church Fathers took it for granted that Holy Communion must be smuggled in and practiced insofar as possible. Cyprian arranged such a service for the elder Lucian. Lucian, lying with his legs wrenched wide apart in the stocks of the prison at Antioch, celebrated Holy Communion for the last time as best he could, with the elements resting on his own beaten breast. He celebrated with his condemned companions lying equally helpless in the dark around him.[3] On the evening of March 6, A.D. 203, at a prison in Charthage, the martyrs of the next day, Perpetua and Felicitas, and their companions, were given a free meal by the authorities. This meal they converted as far as possible into an Agape.[4]

For the practice of Holy Communion a whole congregation in an obscure village at Abilinitina in Africa took the risk of almost certain detection by assembling at the height of the Diocletian persecution in their own town, where they were sure to be discovered, because, as they said in court, Holy Communion had been lacking a long while through the apostasy of their bishop, Fundonus. They could no longer bear the lack of it; therefore, they called on an elder to celebrate – and paid the penalty of their faith to a man.[5]

Holy Communion was the first consideration of the Christian and the Church in times of persecution and imprisonment. To the early Christians, Holy Communion was more precious

[3] Cyprian, *Epistles,* 5. 2.
[4] Tertullian, *Passion of Perpetua and Feliticas.*
[5] *Acta Martyrum Abilinitinensium.*

than their lives. Holy Communion was their ultimate concern because their hope of eternal life was in remembrance of Him who loved them and gave Himself for them. Tertullian answers the question of the practice of Holy Communion, "But how shall we meet, you ask, how shall we celebrate the Lord's solemnities? . . . If you cannot meet by day, there is always the night."[6] St. Dionysius, bishop of Alexandria, wrote, "To other men the present would not seem to be a time for festival (Holy Communion), nor for them is this or any other time of such a nature. I speak not of times of mourning, but even of any time that might be thought especially joyful. Now indeed all is lamentation, and all men mourn, and wailings resound throughout the city because of the number of dead and of those dying day by day. At first they drove us out, and alone we kept our festival (Holy Communion) at that time also, persecuted and put to death by all; and every single spot where we were afflicted became to us a place of assembly for the feast – field, desert, ship, inn, prison; but the brightest of all festivals was kept by the perfect martyrs, when they feasted in heaven."[7]

Just to read these accounts makes one ashamed of our apathy toward the passion of Christ in the celebration of Holy Communion. The Christian who is indifferent to the practice of Holy Communion in complacent twentieth-century churchism has no place beside the first-century Christians and perhaps reveals that he has no place in the Church, nor in the Kingdom of God!

The infinite price paid for immeasurable grace of Holy Communion is the incarnate life of the Son of God. The price paid for our Christian heritage of the faith is also the laying down of life, the life of the martyrs. A letter of Cyprian to the Christian martyrs in the mines reveals the price paid for Holy Communion. "But that, being first severely

[6] Tertullian, *de Fuga in Persecution,* 14.
[7] Dionysius, 2. 4., Eusebius — *Ecclesiastical History,* 7. 22.

beaten with clubs, and ill-used, you have begun by sufferings of that kind, the glorious firstlings of your confession, is not a matter to be execrated by us. For a Christian body is not very greatly terrified at clubs, seeing all its hope is in the WOOD (cross). The servant of Christ acknowledges the *sacrament of his salvation;* redeemed by wood to life eternal, he is advanced by wood to the crown. But what wonder if, as golden and silver vessels, you have committed to the mind that is the home of gold and silver, except that now the nature of the mines is changed, and the places which previously had been accustomed to yield gold and silver have begun to receive them? Moreover, they have put fetters on your feet, and have bound your blessed limbs, and the temples of God with disgraceful chains, as if the spirit also could be bound with the body or your gold could be stained by the contact of iron. To men who are dedicated to God, and who attest their faith with religious courage, such things are ornaments, not chains; nor do they bind the feet of Christians for infamy, but glorify them for a crown. Oh feet blessedly bound, which are loosed, not by the smith but by the Lord! Oh feet blessedly bound, which are guided to paradise in the way of salvation! Oh feet bound for the present time in the world, that they may be always free with the Lord! Oh feet, lingering for a while among the fetters and cross-bars, but to run quickly to Christ on a glorious road! Let cruelty, either envious or malignant, hold you here in its bonds and chains as long as it will; from this earth and from these sufferings you should speedily come to the Kingdom of Heaven. The body is not cherished in the mines with couch and cushion, but it is cherished with the refreshment and solace of Christ. The frame wearied with labours lies prostate on the ground, but it is no penalty to lie down with Christ. . . . There the bread is scarce; but man liveth not by bread alone, but by the Word of God. But there cannot be felt any loss of either religion or faith, most beloved brethren, in the fact that now there is given no opportunity there to God's priests for offering and celebrating the divine sacrifices (sacraments); yea you celebrate and offer a sacrifice to God equally precious and glorious, and that will greatly profit you for the retribution of heavenly rewards, since the sacred Scripture speaks, saying, 'The sacrifice of God is a broken spirit; a contrite and humbled heart God doth not despise.' You offer this sacrifice to God; you celebrate this sacrifice without intermission day and night, being made victims to God, and exhibiting yourselves as holy and unspotted offerings, as the apostle exhorts and says, 'I beseech you therefore, brethren, by the mercies of God, that ye present your bodies a living sacrifice, holy, acceptable unto God. And be not conformed to this world; but be ye transformed by the renewing of your mind, that ye may prove what is that good, and acceptable, and perfect will of God."[8] What a contrast between these early "brethren" who sought the grace of God in Holy Communion at the price of their lives and the Christian today who seeks the grace of God at the price of one hour a week, or two hours a year!

The name Christian is an honorable name bought with the blood of the Son of God and Christian martyrs. What right do we have to cheapen it with callous indifference? Holy Communion is a privilege, not a penalty, to be entered into with the sacredness of the blood of Christian martyrs, and of the blood of the incarnate God in Christ.

The shame and weakness of the Church today is that it has taken the genuine Christian doctrine of justification by faith alone and misused it for the protection and practice of sinful man. The Reformers were perfectly right in refusing to tolerate the Roman Catholic sanction of sinful indulgences and the "sacrificing again" of Christ in the Mass any longer. Luther and the Reformers realized the essence of Christ's Gospel: "The Law and the prophets both bear witness to it:

[8] Cyprian, *To Nemesianus and Other Martyrs in the Mines, Epistle* 76.

it is God's way of righting wrong, effective through faith in Christ for all who have such faith – all, without distinction. For all alike have sinned and are deprived of the divine splendour; all are justified by God's free grace alone, through his act of liberation in the Person of Christ Jesus" (Rom. 3:21-23). Grace is God's only answer for the soul of man. However, this grace is the point where the process of Christian living begins in committed discipleship. The doctrine of justification means the justification of the sinner, not justifying his sins, and when the Christian realizes the amazing grace of God in his life he is driven to become a Christian disciple in a desperate world, witnessing to the amazing love of God in Christ.

The price of Christian discipleship is still the same as in the parable of the Lord, "The kingdom of heaven is like treasure lying buried in a field. The man who found it buried it again, and for sheer joy went and sold everything he had, and bought that field" (Matt. 13:44). The Church has taken up the word of the Reformers and proclaimed "justification by faith alone," but has failed to proclaim the corollary call to Christian living. Because the price of pardon has been paid by Christ on the Cross, it does not free us from the price of giving our lives in decision and dedication. Holy Communion has been purchased with the price of the life of the Son of God; it can be shared only at the price of our committed lives.

The way to God's righteousness is still the chief temptation of the Church. The reformation of society by government, organization, progress, and policies, instead of by the soul's new creation, is still the naive proposal of some. God's grace which makes men just with God is the only basis of making men just with each other. The price of complete Christian dedication is thought too high; thus arises the temptation to save men by rallying their goodness without routing their evil, by re-organizing virtue instead of redeeming guilt. The price of the gift of God's grace has been established by Christ, "My Father, if it be possible, let this cup pass from me: yet not as I will, but as thou wilt" (Matt. 26:39). Christ paid with His life. He has also established the price for sharing the eternal life which he wrought on the Cross: "For whosoever will save his life shall lose it; but whosoever shall lose his life for my sake and the Gospel's, the same shall save it" (Mark 8:35, *KJV*).

The incarnation of God in Christ creates a call to each person which excludes contemplation and demands choice. The revelation of God in the Person of Christ demands obedient faith. God in the incarnate Christ calls us to burn all bridges and follow Him; we are urgently invited to an exclusive attachment to His Person. At the point of the incarnation of God in the Person of Christ, man is brought face to face with God and the choice of "surrendering" to Him and receiving His grace, or being "offended" in Him because in Him man comes to a realization of his utter worthlessness and sinful nature. The call of Christ to each human person transcends all religious laws. It is the summons of loving grace, "follow me." This is the nature of the call to Levi and the reason he "arose and followed Him" (Mark 2:14). The *Person* of God in Christ burst upon him and flooded away all common sense excuses and rational reasons why he should not follow – now. He was confronted with the Absolute, and absolutely surrendered and followed. Christ also confronted James and John. The Scripture is exact in describing Christ's call to James and John, "He went on, and saw another pair of brothers, James son of Zebedee and his brother John; they were in the boat with their father Zebedee, overhauling their nets. He called them, and *at once* (immediately) they left the boat and their father and followed him" (Matt. 4:21, 22). God encountered James and John and imposed upon them the choice to follow or not to follow. It is significant that they left their firm and their father to follow Him. The obedient faith of Levi, James, and John is in contrast to the lack of faith and obedience of the rich young ruler: "Jesus said to him, 'If you wish to go *the whole way*, go, sell your possessions, and give to the poor, and then you will have riches in heaven; and come, follow me.' When the young man heard this, he went away, with a heavy heart . . ." (Matt. 19:21, 22). This would-be Christian recognized Jesus as the Master, but failed to give obedient faith to the personal call of God. The consequence was that rather than follow the absolute call of God into an entirely new realm, he went back to his old creaturely heavy heart. Laying aside all psychological arguments and theological implications, the essential truth of the call of the Person of God in Christ is that faith comes through obedience. God is no longer an abstract idea which can be subjected to empirical proofs, but the divine Person who comes to every human person in grace, and judgment. The question which came first, faith or obedience, loses all meaning in the Person of Christ. The propositions, "Only he who has faith is obedient, and only he who is obedient has faith," are equally true.[9] Levi, James, and John were obedient and believed, and believed and were obedient. The rich young ruler did neither. All argument and contemplation are absorbed in the Person of God in Christ and leave us with a clear choice. The incarnation of the Person of God in Christ eliminates all ultimate choices except one, belief or unbelief in the Lord Jesus Christ.

It is impossible to hear the Gospel and go away the same. Everyone who hears the Gospel is either better or worse, whether he knows it or not. When we are brought to face God in Christ, it is either our salvation or our condemnation. The crucial decisive thing of the world is the Cross of Christ. It alone decided life or death. Our choice is to kneel in submission at the foot of the cross and receive the life of God in Christ, or not to kneel and remain in death. The reason why so many Christian worship services are dull to so many is not just the preacher. The hopefulness and infinite patience with which congregations wait upon preaching is pathetic enough

[9] Bonhoeffer, *op. cit.*, p. 59.

and still more pathetic is the frequency of disappointment. However, more often Christian worship turns upon the miracle of grace of God, which is so great a miracle that it is strange and remote to man's natural way of thinking and living. It is like the dull reading of an instruction book for a country one has never visited and to which one never intends to go. The reason people do not read the Bible more, nor enjoy worship, is that they have not been in the new country, nor is there the experience of grace for it to stir and build upon. We must be shaken to realize that it was God who did His work in Christ, and Christ was the almighty God working upon men.

As believers, our singular purpose is to witness to Him and extend the call of God to follow. Those who are witnessed to are confronted with a choice, not a discussion. The call to Christian discipleship is made absolute, by the Absolute. God paid the absolute and final price of death and sin in the incarnation and crucifixion, and thereby is demanded the necessary, absolute, and final price of surrendering our self-interest and self-wills. The shallowness of Christian faith does not lead to eventual great faith and eternal life, but spawns spiritual death. The Christian's and Church's half-commitment does not provide a flicker of hope in the earth's dark day, but leads to the world's non-commitment. For the world sees the fallacy of half-commitment to the Person of God in Christ and rejects it all. The price is high, life; but the stake is higher, eternal life. This is the sterling value and holy meaning of Holy Communion.

The New Testament scholar, J. B. Phillips, writes, "The man who in his heart intends to go on being selfish or proud, or who has already decided how far his Christian convictions should carry him is probably obeying a sound instinct when he keeps away from this glorious but perilous sacrament. For, if the truth be told, men are often willing to put their trust in a god who in the end must be triumphant, simply because they want to be on the winning side; but they are not nearly so ready to bear any part of the cost of that winning. Yet the fellowship of the broken bread and the poured-out wine can mean no less than that."[10]

In Holy Communion the bread is broken. The bread must be broken; the loaf cannot be eaten whole. So it was a spiritual necessity, a necessity in God, that Christ should die. He should have escaped if He had not felt that He obeyed a divine law which even He could not change, because He could not wish to change it. It was a law of His soul, of His heaven.[11] The ordained principle of God remains intact in Christ, the principle that "In truth, in very truth I tell you, a grain of wheat remains a solitary grain unless it falls into the ground and dies; but if it dies, it bears a rich harvest" (John 12:24). Just as food must be destroyed before it produces life, so Christ had to die before He could be our Savior. Death is the price of spiritual life. As the bread in Holy Communion must be broken before it blesses, so we must be broken before God can bless us. Self-will, self-seeking, self-love must be broken in the grace of God, or else all other Christian worship and contribution is rejected by God. We seek to substitute, to evade, to compromise, to give *things* without giving *self*. But God remains unimpressed and we remain impounded in our sin. As Christ broke the bread at the Last Supper, so He gave His body to be broken on the cross. And as His body was broken so were His heart and will. *Without "the breaking" there is no salvation, nor sharing in salvation.* The price of Holy Communion is His life – and ours.

The price of Christianity is the Cross, not only His, but ours. "Then he called the people as well as his disciples to him and said to them, 'Anyone who wishes to be a follower of mine must leave self behind; he must take up his cross, and come with me' " (Mark 8:34). To take up one's cross

[10] Phillips, J. B., *Appointment with God,* (London: Wyvern Books, 1962), p. 38.

[11] Forsyth, P. T., *The Church and the Sacraments,* (London: Longmans, 1917), p. 225.

is certainly never asceticism, seldom preaching, but always discipleship. Taking one's cross is never suicide, for that would be an expression of sinful self-will. To deny oneself is to be conscious of Christ, and not of self, to see only the Savior who goes before, rather than the hard rough road. *To take up one's cross is to become oblivious to self in allegiance to Christ.* In the fellowship of the crucified and glorified body of Christ we participate in His suffering and glory. His Cross is carried by His body, the Church. Our cross bearing begins at our baptismal death and continues through life, "every day I die" (I Cor. 15:31). Our cross is not mere human suffering, but suffering and rejection related to the Gospel of Christ. We are embarked on a new adventure to a new land which demands our shoving off from the old shore and moving against the tide which constantly flows against our new direction. Our new life by the grace of Him who loved us and gave Himself for us is the compass of our lives and the source of strength to encounter successfully the temptations in the arena of life. This is our cross, the price we pay for Holy Communion.

The price God paid for Holy Communion is described by the prophet Isaiah, "Surely he hath borne our griefs, and carried our sorrows: yet we did esteem him stricken, smitten of God, and afflicted. But he was wounded for our transgressions, he was bruised for our iniquities: the chastisement of our peace was upon him; and with his stripes we are healed" (Isa. 53:4, 5). In this passage the emphasis is upon *our* and *He*. The sublime truth is that in this one Man all men are represented, in this one moment all time is gathered, in this one soul all sin is borne and redeemed. All pain and poverty, misery and malice, guilt and guile, war and wickedness, suffering and sin of all time are borne in Him. Sin is not only personal and individual, but social and collective, and it is the sin of the individual and of the world that Christ is bearing on the Cross. The Cross was no mere martyrdom or miscarriage of human justice, but God's intent and purpose; His voluntary offering was an expiatory sacrifice. The debt of sin was paid, the curse cancelled, and the saved soul brought into a true relationship with God. Such a work could not have been accomplished by a mere martyr, however great, but only by the Son of God. He alone could pay the price, and He alone did pay the price: "The Lord has laid on Him the iniquity of us all" (Isa. 53:6). An old saying runs: "There are three ways in which a man expresses his deep sorrows: The man on the lowest level cries; the man on the second level is silent; the man on the highest level knows how to turn his sorrow into song."[12] The Lord from the Cross turned defeat to victory, hate to love, sin to salvation, and sorrow of death to the joy of resurrected life. The immeasurably high price paid by God in Christ for Holy Communion is the measure of our high privilege in entering into Holy Communion.

When I survey the wondrous Cross
  On which the Prince of Glory died,
My richest gain I count but loss,
  And pour contempt on all my pride.

Forbid it, Lord, that I should boast,
  Save in the death of Christ, my God;
All the vain things that charm me most,
  I sacrifice them through His blood.

See! from His head, His hands, His feet,
  Sorrow and love flow mingled down;
Did e'er such love and sorrow meet,
  Or thorns compose so rich a crown?

Were the whole realm of Nature mine,
  That were an offering far too small,

[12] Muilenburg, James, "Isaiah 40-66," *The Interpreter's Bible,* (New York: Abingdon Press, 1956), Vol. V, p. 621.

Love so amazing, so divine,
Demands my soul, my life, my all.[13]

The Gift of Life

The price is high, life; but the prize is infinitely higher, eternal life. Life is the major theme of the Bible, the essence of the Gospel, and the heart of the Church. Holy Communion must always be regarded from the Easter side of the Cross, resurrected life. It is not a funeral meal, but the joy of celebrating the victory of Christ and the anticipation of the marriage feast of the Lamb. Holy Communion is a thanksgiving meal where His sacrifice is the death unto life. We are guests at His table and thus are not separated by His death upon the Cross, but united with our resurrected and living Lord and Master. Holy Communion is not a mere memorial meal, but an event. "Whosoever believeth on me, *hath* life eternal" (John 3:15). We are already in possession of the prize of life. Our death is already dead, and our life is already eternal life. As guests of His table we are already partaking of eternal life.

The world is eclipsed by death. Death has stung all life with its poison, "the wages of sin is death." Its shadow is present, especially where life shines brightest. Human existence is born to die, branded by death from the beginning. Death is the contradiction continually raised against our existence. Love is separated and purposes are interrupted by this great enemy. A man who has never been terrified by death hasn't yet known the living God. But now the Cross of Christ and His resurrection have removed the sting and poison of death, "Death is swallowed up in victory. O death, where is thy sting? O grave, where is thy victory" (I Cor. 15:54, 55)? We who have come to the revelation of God in Christ have passed through death to life: "I am crucified

[13] Isaac Watts.

with Christ; the life I now live is not my life" (Gal. 2:20). It is the Christian in the world who comes to the reality of death in the realization of the new life. It is the Christian who is the realist, who recognizes the consequence of human existence as death, but resolves it in the new life of God in Christ. The paradox of the faith is that at the point of death in surrender of self-will, we immediately make a one hundred eighty degree turn to eternal life: "If we thus died with Christ, we believe that we shall also come to life with him" (Rom. 6:8). The man who believes that, is already beginning here and now to live the complete life. The Christian hope is the seed of eternal life. In Jesus Christ I am no longer at the point at which I can die; in Him our bodies are already in heaven. Since we have received His testimony in Holy Communion, we already live here and now in anticipation of the life to come, when God will be all in all.[14]

Life is indeed the purpose for which Christ came into the world: "I have come that men may have life" (John 10:10). Life is the purpose for the writing of the Gospel of John, "There were indeed many other signs that Jesus performed in the presence of his disciples, which are not recorded in this book. But these are recorded in order that you may hold the faith that Jesus is the Christ, the Son of God, and that through faith you may possess eternal life by his name" (John 20:31). "Life" (zoa) and "eternal life" belong to the common vocabulary of Christianity. Both terms have roots in the Old Testament, although there the emphasis is on earthly life and well-being. Daniel is an Old Testament book which teaches quite unequivocally the doctrine of a future life (Dan. 12:2). Christ's eternal life is something far more than immortality of the Old Testament. In the story of the raising of Lazarus, Martha expresses the popular view of immortality of Judaism, "I know he will rise again, at the resurrection

[14] Cf. Barth, Karl, "*Dogmatics in Outline,* trans. G. T. Thomson, (London: SCM, 1960), p. 155.

on the last day" (John 11:23, 24). This is the same view expressed earlier in the Gospel, "Do not wonder at this, because the time is coming when all who are in the grave shall hear his voice and move forth: those who have done right will rise to life; those who have done evil will rise to hear their doom" (John 5:28, 29). However, Jesus does not teach simple immortality in answering Martha: "I am the resurrection and I am life. If a man has faith in me, even though he die, he shall come to life; and no one who is alive and has faith shall ever die" (John 11:25, 26). Jesus teaches that eternal life is that which the believer is already living in a pregnant sense, which excludes the possibility of ever ceasing to live. In other words Christ's teaching of the resurrection includes eternal life here and now. This is in harmony with, "In very truth, anyone who gives heed to what I say and puts his trust in him who sent me has hold of eternal life, and does not come up for judgment, but has already passed from death to life" (John 5:24). It is of course true that the believer will enter life at the general resurrection, but to John this is less important than the fact that the believer is already enjoying eternal life.

In the Christian faith life is qualified by "eternal." Eternal is a qualitative rather than a quantitative aspect. The chief thing about it is its difference in quality from mere physical life. Its everlastingness is a function of its divine quality. The eternal life of the Christian faith is not simply the continuing of this present human existence, but the completion of this life in the new creation, "For this corruptible must put on incorruption, and this mortal must put on immortality" (I Cor. 15:53, *KJV*). As the Apostle further describes eternal life, "The first man, Adam, became an animate being; whereas the last Adam has become a life-giving spirit. The man made of dust is the pattern of all men of dust, and the heavenly man is the pattern of all heavenly" (I Cor. 15:45, 47, 48). Our eternal life began the moment the Holy Spirit regenerated us into the new creation of Christ. At that moment our human existence changed from a primary to a secondary value and has no ultimate consequence. The grace of God has shattered the pattern of human existence, life-death, and has established eternal life. The Christian does pass through the death of human existence, just as he has passed through the death of his self-will, but the next existence is always immediate, and "life" is always present. On the other hand, eternal damnation is the continuation of the old Adam in the old sin-cursed, diseased nature in isolation from God and all His goodness, love, and mercy. The first nature of man, human existence, is under the curse of sin, death, and hell, and simply remains so unless changed by the grace of God in regeneration. Eternal damnation is not the state where God arbitrarily places man, but the state in which man freely chooses to remain by his refusal to have obedient faith in Christ and His new life. In view of this, what else can we do but sing the praises of God for the gift of eternal life, and give our lives a living sacrifice. The Lord set forth the point in the parable, "A merchant looking out for the pearls found one of special value; so he went and sold everything he had, and bought it" (Matt. 13:45, 46). The prize of new life has been bought by the precious blood of our Lord; ours is but to receive this gift of eternal life through faith in Him.

The Cross of Christ is the supreme proof of the love of God, and it is also Christ's glory and exaltation. It is sacrificial in character. Christ in Himself is our advocate in the expiation for our sin and the sin of the world. All that has been done in the Christ event is to be appropriated by faith. In Holy Communion the believer feeds upon Him. He is the vine; we are the branches. The Holy Spirit has borne witness with our spirits that God has given us eternal life and that this life is in the Son: "He that hath the Son possesses the life indeed, and he that possesses not the Son of God has not that life" (I John 5:12). The gift of eternal life is in the hands of Christ, and in the hearts of believers in whom the Spirit of Christ dwells as Lord and Savior.

God's gift of life is born of His love. The love of God

which has given life is not facile or cheap. God does not love indiscriminately in the sense of ignoring our sinfulness. God's love is to act, "a consuming fire," to do for man what he cannot do for himself. As D. M. Baillie writes, "The love that draws us near Thee is hot with wrath to them. God must be inexorable towards our sins; not because He is just, but because He is loving; not in spite of His love, but because of His love; not because His love is limited but because it is unlimited and because nothing is inexorable but love."[15] The Apostle describes our life in the love of God in the great climax, "With all this in mind, what are we to say? . . . It is Christ – Christ who died, and, more than that, was raised from the dead – who is at God's right hand, and indeed pleads our cause . . . overwhelming victory is ours through him who loved us. For I am convinced that there is nothing in death or life – nothing in all creation that can separate us from the love of God in Christ Jesus our Lord" (Rom. 8:31-39). Our life born of the love of God is infinitely precious, cherished above all human existence, the crowning prize of life.

The cherished gift of eternal life presupposes something as infinitely precious, the forgiveness of sins and fellowship with God. Repentance, forgiveness, justification, sanctification, reconciliation, and atonement are all equally inseparable from the one central and compendious Christ event. They all must be held in true value and perspective in a worthwhile Christian theology, in a genuine Christian faith. It is the forgiveness of sins and the fellowship with the loving heavenly Father that is most apprehensible and best understood by Christians. "Thy sins be forgiven thee" are the words that continually echo with joy in the believer's heart. The truths of justification, sanctification, reconciliation, and atonement are a necessary part of the Christian doctrine. But the simple words, "God be merciful to me a sinner," and "man, thy sins are forgiven thee" are cherished above all

[15] Baillie, D. M., *op. cit.*, p. 123.

existing words. Forgiveness of sins, resurrection, and eternal life are the Christian's cherished "prize" in Christ.

Perhaps our contemporary world does not seek after or appreciate this prize of the Christian faith. To a degree modern man has lost his sense of sin, dismissing it as "a psychopathic aspect of adolescent mentality."[16] Our society seeks to eradicate sin, without the power and grace of God. It is suggested that the concept of sin is of the past, and the concept of self-sufficiency is for the future. The seriousness and consequence of sin are overshadowed by an affluent sophisticated society. One reason for saying that our society has lost the sense of sin is the fact that if there were a serious sense of sin in our society and in the church, there would be a serious seeking for the forgiveness of God. Theorists may be able to persuade man that he is innocent and that society is self-sufficient; however, the indictment still stands, "The history of the world is the judgment of the world." To any person who thinks honestly and seriously the hard fact of wars and rumors of wars shatters the concept of the innocency of man and the sufficiency of society. Isn't it rather evident that the ominous shadows of the world are the unequivocal signs of the sinfulness of mankind, and that the goodness of God in Christ is the restraint that prevents total self-destruction? The Evangelist John is quick to tell the world in no uncertain words, "If we claim to be sinless, we are self-deceived and strangers to the truth. If we confess our sins, he is just, and may be trusted to forgive our sins and cleanse us from every kind of wrong; but if we say we have committed no sin, we make him out to be a liar, and then his word has no place in us" (I John 1:8, 10).

The initial and constant prayer of the believer is, "Forgive us our trespasses." The Christian has a sense of sin, a true understanding of himself, and a basic knowledge of life

[16] Quoted by Niebuhr, R., *The Nature and Destiny of Man,* (New York: Scribner's and Sons, 1943), p. 100.

and the world. All of this is gained at the Cross. Here we realize that it was necessary for the power of God in Christ to terminate the power of sin, and that we are totally dependent upon Him. God in Christ on the Cross is the only true revelation and evaluation of sin. Here our secret motives are exposed; paralyzing sins are broken, and the proper values of life are established. It is in this process of believing and living in Christ that we become even more grateful for God's forgiveness of sins.

The New Testament does not teach that Christ was crucified in order that God can forgive sins. The forgiveness of sins is an act of God's free grace, and it is He who sets aside the enmity and partitions raised by our sins and makes possible our reconciliation to Himself. Jesus Christ on Calvary is the amazing revelation of a pardoning God. Just as the children of Israel looked upon the brazen serpent in the wilderness, so we look up to the Cross of Christ and are healed. Saving faith is the response to the manifestation of God's love on the Cross. When faith and love meet, reconciliation is effected, and we enter into fellowship with God. Then we sing with the Psalmist, "Out of the depths have I cried unto thee, O Lord. But there is forgiveness with thee . . . I wait for the Lord, my soul doth wait, and in his word do I hope" (Ps. 130:1, 4, 5).

Our fellowship and communion with God that have been bought with the price of His Cross are not to be taken frivolously. To worship rarely, to pray passively, to sing without joy, to cast criticism at the Church, to commune without real repentance, or to be indifferent to it all, are sins against our friendship with God. No wonder the Scriptures teach, "For he who eats and drinks eats and drinks judgment on himself if he does not discern the Body" (I Cor. 11:29). The costly reconciliation of man with God by the Cross is the basis of the stern warning, "For when men have once been enlightened, when they have had a taste of the heavenly gift and share in the Holy Spirit, when they have experienced the goodness of God's word and the Spiritual energies of the age to come, and after all this have fallen away, it is impossible to bring them to repentance, for with their own hands they are crucifying the Son of God and making mock of his death" (Heb. 6:4-6). The fellowship with God is the infinite gift to be cherished in our lives continually.

The term *koinonia* is distinctive, not only in that it means communion, but fellowship with Christ. To be "in Christ" is to have fellowship with Christ who died and arose again, a fellowship so close that we live, die and rise together with Him. Fellowship, the fruit of reconciliation, is not to be spoiled. Fellowship with God is the distinction of the believer from the nonbeliever. Our uniqueness is not in the fact that we are above temptation, sin, suffering, pain, or death, but that we share in the friendship of God.

Holy Communion means change of relation between man and God, man individually and corporately. It is a change of relation from alienation to communion, not simply to our peace and pleasure, but to reciprocal communion. The grand end of atonement and reconciliation, the Christian faith, is Holy Communion. It is not enough that we should simply pay homage to God. It is not enough that we simply respect the Person of God in Christ. It is not enough that we worship the almighty God in an unregenerate humanism. Homage and uncommitted worship do not answer to God, or satisfy the soul of man. Nothing short of living, loving, holy, habitual communion between Himself and our souls can realize at last the end which God achieved in the Lord Jesus Christ.

When we reflect upon Holy Communion, "What have I done?" We should say to ourselves, I have tasted of the future glory of God; I have yielded myself to take part in His finished act of redemption; I have communed with the Holy Eternal God; all of which is greater than the creation of the world.

Epilogue

This short section is somewhat of a postscript, however it might well be the most important part of the whole study. The avenue of study has brought us to a certain pinnacle from which we have a clear retrospect of the awe-inspiring mystery of Holy Communion. Searching the "soul" of the sacramental symbols has established an advantage point which reveals a certain truth for the Church today.

The twentieth-century Church will find the spiritual reformation that is being sought by placing Holy Communion at the center of worship. The early Church experienced dynamic fellowship around the Communion table. The *ecclesia* gathered in the guest chambers of private homes and worshiped the resurrected Christ through the central act of Communion. "Simple in its origin, it quickly became the gathering point of all the deepest invitations and spiritual discoveries."[17] The power of the early Church was the Eucharist, not ecclesiology. The very life of the early Church revolved around the "Love-feast."

The existence of Christianity among all nations now requires a personal and yet universal meeting ground – Holy Communion. The fellowship of men under God is expressed in the Agape; the intimacy of the Spirit finds its way in the Eucharist. Here the uninitiated enters into the clear invitation of grace and focuses his worship on the central act of God. He apprehends what he cannot comprehend. The educated can in the same service contemplate the mysteries of life and God. All levels of society can find the full expression of their faith and understanding of God at Holy Communion. True Communion transcends, embraces, and unites all believers who lay claim to Him, "who loved us and gave Himself for us."

Christians everywhere have a common bond in Holy Com-

[17] Underhill, *op. cit.*, p. 121.

munion. Perhaps the Pedilavium and the Agape, as well as the Eucharist, are the means for the real unity of God's people. The Church historian Donald Durnbaugh writes, "World Church circles are finding great possibilities in the Love-feast, which a writer in *Inter-communion* notes 'may yet prove to be the point at which the divided churches of Christendom may meet in a common act of worship and fellowship.' "[18] The Pedilavium might well be the means to unbend our sophisticated society, our cultured Church. Christian worship can never be divorced from sacrifice, and only when the believer is willing to give himself without reservation is faith operative.

The Church's probing for "the answer" today might well be resolved at the Lord's table. Many local and national church programs planned by countless committees produce little but weariness. The energy, time, and money consumed on "programs" is frightening, and appalling. Holy Communion affords the richness of the ritual and the significance of the Gospel necessary for the Church Universal. The Lord provided the simple and yet profound service for the peoples of the world. Adoration, confession, thanksgiving, and supplication all have a place in Communion. The Christian ritualists and the Christian Biblicists may be seated comfortably at the Lord's table. Proclamation and ritual are both a part of Holy Communion. The spiritual presence of Christ through faith is realized in these sacramental symbols by Christians of every nation.

The timeless Gospel will be relevant to the age only when the members of the body of Christ enter into Communion with Him. The end of the fragmented family of God on earth can come to pass through the common acceptance of this

[18] Durnbaugh, Donald F., "Will The Brethren Prevail," *Brethren Life and Thought,* X (Winter, 1965), p. 61.

divine appointment. The compelling power of Communion transcends all reasoned ecclesiology. The Communion table of our Lord is the singular place of fellowship for the Church. The Love-feast is the natural setting for "brethren" in Christ to gather as the body of Christ.

Bibliography

Baillie, Donald M. *God Was in Christ.* London: Faber and Faber, 1961.

———. *The Theology of the Sacraments.* London: Faber and Faber, 1961.

Baillie, John. *The Place of Jesus Christ in Modern Christianity.* Edinburgh: T. & T. Clark, 1929.

Barclay, William. *A New Testament Workbook.* London: SCM Press, 1955.

Barrett, C. K. *The Gospel According to St. John.* London: S.P.C.K., 1955.

Barth, Karl. *Church Dogmatics.* eds. G. W. Bromiley and T. F. Torrance, 4 vols.; Edinburgh: T. & T. Clark, 1956-62.

———. *Dogmatics in Outline.* Trans. G. T. Thomson. London: SCM Press, 1952.

Begg, Charles. *Epistles of St. Peter and St. Jude.* I.C.C. Edinburgh: T. & T. Clark, 1901.

Bonhoeffer, Dietrich. *The Cost of Discipleship.* London: SCM Press, 1959.

Bouquet, A. C. *Everyday Life in New Testament Times.* London: Batsford, 1954.

Briggs, C. A. *The Book of Psalms.* I.C.C. Edinburgh: T. & T. Clark, 1907.

Bruce, F. F. *The Acts of the Apostles.* London: Tyndale Press, 1951.

Bruce, Robert. *The Mystery of the Lord's Supper.* Trans. T. F. Torrance. Edinburgh: T. & T. Clark, reprint 1958.

Brunner, H. Emil. *The Mediator.* Trans. Olive Wyon. London: Lutterworth Press, 1934.

Bultmann, Rudolf. *Jesus Christ and Mythology.* London: SCM Press, 1958.

———. *Jesus and the Word.* Trans. Louise Pettibone and Erminie Huntress. New York: Scribner's Company, 1934.

Calvin, John. *Commentary on the Gospel According to John.* Trans. W. Pringle. Grand Rapids: Eerdmans, 1949.

Collingwood, R. C. *Speculum Mentis.* Oxford: Clarendon Press, 1924.

Cullmann, Oscar. *Early Christian Worship.* Trans. J. B. Torrance and A. S. Todd. London: SCM Press, 1959.

Curnock, Nehemiah (ed.). *The Journal of John Wesley.* 6 vols., London: Kelly Company, 1938.

Dalman, Gustof. *Jesus-Jesha.* London: S.P.C.K. Press, 1929.

De Vaux, Roland. *Ancient Israel.* London: Darton, Longman & Todd, 1961.

Dillstone, F. W. *Christianity and Symbolism.* London: Collins, 1955.

Dix Gregory. *The Shape of the Liturgy.* Westminster: Dacre Press, 1955.

Dodd, C. H. *The Apostolic Preaching and its Developments.* London: Hodder & Stoughton, 1944.

———. *The Interpretation of the Fourth Gospel.* Cambridge: University Press, 1953.

Edersheim, Alfred. *The Temple.* London: James Clark, 1959.

Forsyth, P. T. *The Church and the Sacraments.* London: Longmans, 1917.

———. *The Person and Place of Jesus Christ.* London: Independent Press, 1946.

Gardner. *A History of Sacraments.* London: Williams and Nargate, 1921.

Grant, Frederick G. *The Gospel of John.* New York: Harper and Brothers, 1956.

Greeves, Frederic. *Theology and the Cure of Souls.* New York: Channel Press Inc., 1960.

Hastings, James (ed.). *Dictionary of the Bible.* 4 vols.; Edinburgh: T. & T. Clark, 1905.

Higgins, J. B. *The Lord's Supper in the New Testament.* London: SCM Press, 1960.

Jeremias, J. *The Eucharistic Words of Jesus.* Oxford: Basil Blackwell, 1955.

Keating, J. F. *The Agape and the Christ.* London: Methuen & Co., 1901.

Kirkpatrick, A. F. *Psalms.* London: Cambridge University Press, 1910.

Lecky, William. *History of European Morals.* London: Longmans, Green Company, 1902.

Lenski, R. C. H. *St. John's Gospel.* Columbus: Lutheran Book Concern, 1942.

Lightfoot, R. H. *St. John's Gospel.* London: Clarendon Press, 1956.

Luth, Walter, *St. John's Gospel.* Richmond: John Knox Press, 1960.

MacGregor, G. H. C. *Eucharistic Origins.* London: Clarke, 1928.

Mackintosh, H. R. *The Doctrine of the Person of Jesus Christ.* Edinburgh: T. & T. Clark, 1912.

McIntyre, John. *On the Love of God.* London: Collins, 1962.

Muedeking, George. *Emotional Problems and the Bible,* Philadelphia: Muhlenberg Press, 1956.

Niebuhr, Reinhold, *The Nature and Destiny of Man.* New York: Charles Scribner's Sons, 1943.

Northcotem, J. and W. R. Brownlow, *Roma Sotterranea.* London: Longmans, 1879.

Nygren, Anders. *Agape and Eros.* London: S.P.C.K., 1953.

Owen, H. P. *Revelation and Existence.* Cardiff: University of Wales Press, 1957.

Paul, Robert S. *The Atonement and the Sacraments.* London: Hodder and Stoughton, 1961.

Phillips, J. B. *Appointment with God.* London: Wyvern Books, 1962.

Plummer, A. *St. John.* Cambridge: University Press, 1890.

Quick, O. C. *The Christian Sacraments.* London: Nisbitt and Co., 1927.

Ramseyer, J. P. *A Companion to the Bible.* New York: Oxford University Press, 1958.

Richardson, C. G. *Zwingli and Cranmer on the Eucharist,* Evanston, Ill.: Seabury Seminary, 1949.

Robert, A. and J. Donaldson (eds.). *The Ante-Nicene Fathers.* 10 vols. New York: Charles Scribner's Sons, 1925.

Schaff, Philip and Henry Wace (eds.). *A Select Library of Nicene and Post-Nicene Fathers.* New York: Charles Scribner's Sons, 1886-1890.

Schaff, Philip. *The Creeds of Christendom.* 3 vols. New York: Harper and Brothers, 1877.

Taylor, Vincent. *Forgiveness and Reconciliation.* London: Macmillan & Co., 1946.

————. *Jesus and His Sacrifice.* London: Macmillan & Co., 1951.

————. *The Names of Jesus.* London: Macmillan & Co., 1953.

Torrance, T. F. *Conflict and Agreement in the Church.* London: Lutterworth Press, 1960.

Underhill, Evelyn. *Worship,* New York: Harper & Brothers, 1957.

Vokes, F. E. *The Riddle of the Didache.* New York: Macmillan & Company, 1938.

Wallace, R. S. *Calvin's Doctrine of the Word and Sacrament.* Edinburgh: Oliver and Boyd, 1953.

Wallis, Charles L. *The Table of the Lord.* New York: Harper & Brothers, 1958.

Westcott, G. F. *The Gospel According to St. John.* London: Murray, 1908.

Wotherspoon, H. J. *Religious Values in the Sacraments.* Edinburgh: T. & T. Clark, 1928.

Yoder, C. F. *God's Means of Grace,* Elgin, Ill.: Brethren Publishing House, 1908.

PERIODICALS

Durnbaugh, Donald F. "Will The Brethren Prevail," *Brethren Life and Thought.* Winter, 1965.

MacGregor, G. H. C. "The Eucharist in the Fourth Gospel," *New Testament Studies.* January, 1963.

Wiemer, Glen. "Symbols in Religious Practice," *Brethren Life and Thought.* Autumn, 1959.